IPHONE 15

PRO CAMERA

USER GUIDE

A Complete Guide To Digital Photography & Videography For Professional Content Creator, Beginners And Seniors With Tips & Tricks For iOS 17 Camera

By

Williams M. Brown

© **Copyright 2024 Williams M. Brown**

All rights reserved. No part of this book shall be reproduced, stored in a retrieval system, or transmitted by any means, electronic, mechanical, photocopying, recording, or otherwise, without written permission from the publisher. Although every precaution has been taken in the preparation of this book, the publisher and author assume no responsibility for errors or omissions. Nor is any liability assumed for damages resulting from the use of the information contained herein.

Table Of Contents

INTRODUCTION 11
CHAPTER ONE 35
THE IPHONE CAMERA BASICS 35
    SWITCH BETWEEN CAMERA MODES 37
    ZOOM IN OR ZOOM OUT 38
  HOW TO USE IPHONE CAMERA TO SET UP YOUR SHOT 38
    MODIFY THE EXPOSURE AND FOCUS OF THE CAMERA. 39
    UTILIZE THE TIMER 42
    TO ENSURE A PERFECTLY LEVEL PHOTO, USE A GRID. 42
CHAPTER TWO 44
HOW TO MASTER THE CAMERA APP ON IPHONE 15 PRO 44
    USING THE ON-SCREEN CONTROLS TO MASTER THE IPHONE 15 PRO CAMERA APP 48
    THE IPHONE 15 PRO AND 15 PRO MAX'S ZOOM LEVELS 50
    GETTING THE MOST OUT OF YOUR IPHONE 15 PRO'S CAMERA APP: EXTRA FEATURES, OPTIONS, AND CONTROLS 52

3

HOW TO MASTER THE CAMERA APP ON IPHONE 15 PRO- EXTRA SHOOTING MODES 55
CHAPTER THREE 62
HOW TO SET PHOTOGRAPHIC STYLES ON IPHONE CAMERA 62
- HOW TO SET PHOTOGRAPHIC STYLES ON IPHONE 63
- HOW TO TAKE LIVE PHOTOS 69
  - HOW TO VIEW AND EDIT LIVE PHOTO 70
  - RESTORE THE ORIGINAL LIVE PHOTO 72
  - STATIC IMAGE CONVERSION FROM LIVE PHOTO 72
  - HOW TO SHARE LIVE PHOTOS 73
  - HOW TO TURN OFF LIVE PHOTOS TEMPORARILY 75
  - HOW TO DISABLE LIVE PHOTOS 76
  - THINGS TO KNOW BEFORE DISABLING LIVE PHOTOS 78

CHAPTER FOUR 80
HOW TO TAKE PORTRAITS WITH YOUR IPHONE CAMERA 80
- TAKE A PORTRAIT IN PORTRAIT MODE ... 81

ADJUST DEPTH CONTROL IN PORTRAIT MODE 83

MODIFY THE LIGHTING FOR A PORTRAIT WHILE IN PORTRAIT MODE 84

TAKE A PORTRAIT IN PHOTO MODE 85

HOW TO USE THE IPHONE TO EDIT PORTRAITS 86

MODIFY THE LIGHTING EFFECT FOR PORTRAITS 87

MODIFY PORTRAIT DEPTH CONTROL 89

ADJUST A PORTRAIT'S FOCAL LENGTH 90

USE THE PORTRAIT FILTER ON IMAGES CAPTURED IN THE CAMERA'S PICTURE MODE. 91

CHAPTER FIVE 92

HOW TO TAKE PANORAMA PHOTOS WITH IPHONE 92

METHODS FOR MAINTAINING A STABLE IPHONE 93

THE IMPORTANCE OF HOME PRACTICE FOR IPHONE PANORAMAS 94

METHODS FOR CREATING PANORAMAS ON AN IPHONE 96

HOW TO BREAK COMPOSITION RULES FOR MORE CREATIVE PHOTOS 97

WHY YOU SHOULD AVOID MOVING OBJECTS 98

HOW TO TAKE A SELFIE ON IPHONE CAMERA 99

IMPROVING YOUR SELFIES WITH THE IPHONE CAMERA APP 101

HOW TO TAKE A GOOD SELFIE 103

CHAPTER SIX 106

HOW TO TAKE MACRO PHOTOS AND VIDEOS WITH YOUR IPHONE CAMERA 106

DOCUMENT THE SUBJECT WITH A CLOSE-UP SHOT OR VIDEO 106

TAKE A MACRO SLOW-MOTION OR TIME-LAPSE VIDEO 106

CONTROL AUTOMATIC MACRO SWITCHING 107

HOW TO USE NIGHT MODE CAMERA ON IPHONE 108

5 TIPS FOR GETTING THE BEST NIGHT MODE SHOTS 112

HOW TO TAKE APPLE PRORAW PHOTOS WITH YOUR IPHONE CAMERA 116

SET UP APPLE PRORAW 117

TAKE A PHOTO WITH APPLE PRORAW 117

MODIFY THE PRE-SET FORMAT AND RESOLUTION OF APPLE PRORAW. 118

CHAPTER SEVEN 119

HOW TO RECORD VIDEOS WITH YOUR IPHONE CAMERA 119

RECORD A VIDEO 119

TAKE HIGH-DEFINITION OR ULTRA-HIGH-DEFINITION FOOTAGE. 120

TURN ON ACTION MODE. 120

CAPTURE A VIDEO WITH QUICKTAKE 121

CAPTURE A VIDEO IN SLOW MOTION 124

HOW TO TAKE A SCREEN RECORDING ON IPHONE 125

HOW TO USE THE APPLE PRORES ON THE IPHONE 126

RECORD VIDEO IN APPLE PRORES 126

MANAGE PRORES FILES 130

USE THE PRORES WITH PHOTOS AND OTHER APPS 132

SHARE PRORES VIDEO 133

7

HOW TO USE CINEMATIC MODE ON YOUR IPHONE 134

    HOW TO RECORD VIDEO IN CINEMATIC MODE 135

    EDIT VIDEO TAKEN IN CINEMATIC MODE 136

    HOW TO ADJUST HDR SETTINGS ON IPHONE 140

CHAPTER EIGHT 142

HOW TO TURN OFF THE CAMERA SOUND ON IPHONE 142

    USING ASSISTIVE TOUCH WITHOUT THE RINGER OR SILENT RELAY 145

    DECREASE CAMERA CLICK VOLUME: MUTE THE CLICK-CLICK-CLICK 148

    HOW TO CHANGE THE CAMERA'S VIDEO RECORDING SETTINGS ON IPHONE 150

    ALTER THE VIDEO'S FRAME RATE AND RESOLUTION WITH THE PUSH OF A BUTTON. 150

    ADJUST THE AUTO FPS SETTINGS 151

    TURN STEREO RECORDING ON AND OFF 151

    ACTIVATE AND DEACTIVATE HIGH DYNAMIC RANGE (HDR) VIDEO. 151

8

ALTER THE STATE OF THE LOCK CAMERA. 152

TOGGLE THE SWITCH FOR ENHANCED STABILIZATION. 152

DEACTIVATE AND ACTIVATE THE LOCK WHITE BALANCE 153

CHAPTER NINE 154

WHAT IS LIVE TEXT ON IPHONE 154

HOW TO ACTIVATE LIVE TEXT 154

HOW TO SEARCH A DICTIONARY OR ONLINE 159

HOW TO VIEW PHOTOS AND VIDEOS SHARED WITH YOU ON IPHONE 162

CHAPTER TEN 164

HOW TO MAKE A FACETIME CALL ON IPHONE 164

HOW TO MAKE A NEW FACETIME CALL. 164

HOW TO TURN OFF VIDEO OR MUTE YOURSELF WHILE ON A FACETIME CALL 166

MAKING A FACETIME CALL LINK ON DEVICES OTHER THAN APPLE 167

HOW TO MAKE A FACETIME AUDIO OR VIDEO CALL ON IOS 14 AND OLDER 168

9

HOW TO SWITCH FROM A REGULAR CALL TO FACETIME ON YOUR IPHONE............. 169

HOW TO TURN OFF VIDEO WHILE ON A FACETIME CALL ON IOS 14 AND OLDER . 170

HOW TO USE SIRI TO PLACE A FACETIME CALL 171

HOW TO USE FACETIME WITH APPLE TV 172

CHAPTER ELEVEN 174

HOW TO ORGANIZE PHOTOS ON IPHONE 174

    ADDING PHOTOS TO CUSTOM ALBUMS .. 177

    REMOVING DUPLICATE OR UNWANTED PHOTOS 192

    MANAGING THE RECENTLY DELETED ALBUM 197

    USING ICLOUD FOR PHOTO SYNC AND SHARING 198

CHAPTER TWELVE 200

TIPS AND TRICKS 200

INTRODUCTION

There was a time when the iPhone Pro Max, Apple's priciest flagship, was your only option for a plus-sized iPhone. Luckily, it wasn't an isolated incident; last year, Apple modified when it replaced the iPhone small with the new iPhone 14 Plus.

In keeping with that pattern, Apple has released the iPhone 15 Plus this year, which has several noteworthy upgrades that need a more thorough examination. The 6.1-inch iPhone 15, which is less expensive, and the more feature-rich iPhone 15 Pro continue to occupy the same uncomfortable middle ground. Is it worth it to go for the bigger and better, or would you be better off with Apple's more compact flagship? Come on, we're going to compare the two.

iPhone 15 Pro Vs. iPhone 15 Plus: Specs

	iPhone 15 Pro	iPhone 15 Plus
Size	146.6 x 70.6 x 8.25mm (5.77 x 2.78 x 0.32 inches)	160.9 x 77.8 x 7.8mm (6.33 x 3.0(
Weight	187 grams (6.60 ounces)	201 grams (7.09 ounces)
Screen	6.1-inch always-on Super Retina XDR OLED with 120Hz ProMotion	6.7-inch Super Retina XDR OLEI
Screen resolution	2556 x 1179 pixels at 460 pixels-per-inch	2796 x 1290 pixels at 460 pixels
Operating system	iOS 17	iOS 17
Storage	128GB, 256GB, 512GB, 1TB	128GB, 256GB, 512GB
MicroSD card slot	No	No
Tap-to-pay services	Apple Pay	Apple Pay
Processor	Apple A17 Pro	Apple A16 Bionic
Camera	Rear: 48-megapixel (MP) main camera (wide), 12MP Ultrawide, 12MP telephoto, LiDAR Scanner Front: 12MP TrueDepth	Rear: 48-megapixel (MP) main c 12MP ultrawide Front: 12MP TrueDepth

Video	4K at 24/25/30/60 frames per second (fps) 1080p HD at 25/30/60 fps HDR video with Dolby Vision up to 4K at 60fps Slow motion 1080p at 120/240 fps ProRes video recording up to 4K at 60fps with external recording Macro video recording	4K at 24/25/30/60 frames per se 1080p HD at 25/30/60 fps HDR video with Dolby Vision up t Slow motion 1080p at 120/240 fp
Cellular	5G mmWave (U.S. models only) 5G (sub-6GHz), Dual eSIM with Physical SIM on non-U.S. models only.	5G mmWave (U.S. models only) 5 6GHz), Dual eSIM with Physical S U.S. models only.
Bluetooth version	Bluetooth 5.3	Bluetooth 5.3
Ports	USB-C	USB-C

Water resistance	IP68	IP68
Battery	Video playback: 20 to 23 hours Audio playback: 75 hours 20W fast charging	Video playback: 20 to 26 hours Audio playback: 100 hours 20W fast charging
App marketplace	App Store	App Store
Network support	All major carriers	All major carriers
Colors	Natural Titanium, Blue Titanium, White Titanium, Black Titanium	Blue, Pink, Yellow, Green, Black
Price	Starting at $999	Starting at $899

iPhone 15 Pro Vs. iPhone 15 Plus: Design

Titanium reigns supreme in Apple's iPhone 15 Pro lineup this year. Compared to their stainless steel predecessors, the two premium variants are much lighter and have a brushed metallic finish.

This has practical implications since it means the iPhone 15 Pro is now lighter than the iPhone 15 Plus. The weight difference between last year's iPhone 14 Pro and 14 Plus is puzzling given the variance in screen size. However, compared to last year's iPhone 15 Plus, this year's iPhone 15 Pro is noticeably 14 grams lighter.

There are more than simply weight-related aesthetic differences. A range of muted tones, including Natural, Blue, White, and Black Titanium, are available for the iPhone 15 Pro, in keeping with Apple's titanium philosophy. The iPhone 15 Plus, in contrast, is available in a rainbow of pastel hues beyond just black, including blue, pink, green, and yellow. It is an all-metal device, after all.

The absence of a (PRODUCT) RED model from the regular iPhone range is a first since 2019, and the remaining hues aren't exactly eye-catching either. Even while Apple now uses a different method to infuse the color into the rear glass, giving it a deeper, matte appearance, the pastels are still easily identifiable, and one might easily mistake Apple's "blue" for a silvery-white.

On the other hand, the ergonomics of the new iPhone 15 Plus are the most striking design element. Not like Apple's earlier plus-sized iPhones, which made you feel like you were lugging around a brick, this one strikes a better balance and has slightly rounded edges. Apple has also done this with its titanium iPhone 15 Pro, but the 6.1-inch devices were already rather slim, so although it's apparent on both iPhones, the 15 Plus has it far worse.

To further broaden accessory compatibility and eliminate the need for dongles, the whole iPhone 15 series has switched to the industry-standard USB-C connection from Apple's proprietary Lightning port. It's an improvement, but the port is still on the bottom of the iPhone, so there's no meaningful change to the aesthetic.

The iPhone 15 Pro and iPhone 15 Plus have the same IP68 water-resistant certification as every other iPhone from Apple since the 2020 iPhone 12 series. They can be immersed in water for up to 30 minutes and are resistant to a wide variety of common beverages, including soda, beer, coffee, tea, juice, and more. Even though Apple's Ceramic Shield glass covers the front of both smartphones, they are just as durable as each other. The rear of the iPhone 15 Pro remains standard glass, even if it is titanium.

The design of the iPhone 15 Plus and the iPhone 15 Pro will be determined by aspects such as screen size and personal desire. Because of the lack of consensus on any other factor, we will declare a tie in terms of build quality and durability.

iPhone 15 Pro Vs. iPhone 15 Plus: Display

There are two noticeable improvements to the display of the iPhone 15 Plus when compared to the model released in 2022. All iPhone 15 models now have access to the Dynamic Island feature, which was previously introduced on the iPhone 14 Pro. This is the first and most visible change.

Although it could go unnoticed at first, the screen on the iPhone 15 Plus is much brighter. The screen's maximum brightness has been increased to 1,600 nits in HDR mode and 2,000 nits when used outdoors.

This is why the iPhone 15 Plus's screen is so identical to the iPhone 15 Pro's; both devices retain the same peak brightness and Dynamic Island settings as last year's iPhone 14 Pro. Aside from the obvious size difference, you won't notice any difference between the two screens at first glance. The True Tone display, 460 ppi density, and wide P3 color gamut OLED screens made by Apple are identical to the two handsets.

But, as compared to the iPhone 15 Pro, the adaptive refresh rate—which makes the always-on display possible—gains a substantial advantage. The Always-On Display feature is absent from the iPhone 15 Plus and the screen's fixed 60 Hz resolution remains unchanged, in contrast to the 15 Pro Display's ability to go from 10 to 120 Hz under normal operation and down to 1 Hz forever.

This is from the ProMotion technology developed by Apple. Reducing the refresh rate to 24 or 30 Hz to match the frame rate of whatever you're seeing increases battery life for streaming video and enhances compatibility for fast-paced action games. It also delivers silky-smooth scrolling.

You can't have it both ways—a larger screen with 60Hz or a smaller screen with a faster, always-on display. The difference is large enough to make choosing between the two models challenging. Since physical dimensions aren't everything and a 60Hz screen on an iPhone 15 Pro sounds like a steal in 2023, we're leaning toward that model.

iPhone 15 Pro Vs. iPhone 15 Plus: Performance And Battery

When it comes to performance, there is no competitor to either the iPhone 15 Pro or the iPhone

15 Plus. The most expensive iPhone models now utilize only Apple's top-tier central processing units, which is why. All models of the iPhone 14 were upgraded to the A16 Bionic last year, except the Pro variants, which stuck with the fundamental A15 components from the 13 Pro from 2021.

Compared to their last separation, Apple has stepped it up this time. Apple has renamed the new A-series CPU in the iPhone 15 Pro as the A17 Pro and removed the "Bionic" name since it is so much superior to the one in the iPhone 15 Plus from last year.

All signs point to the iPhone 15 Pro being a gaming behemoth thanks to its redesigned graphics processing unit (GPU), which includes features like hardware-accelerated ray-tracing and is made utilizing modern 3-nanometer technology. App Store exclusives on the iPhone 15 Pro and iPhone 15 Pro Max include titles like Resident Evil Village, which are console exclusives. Several exclusive titles are on the way, including Assassin's Creed: Mirage from Ubisoft.

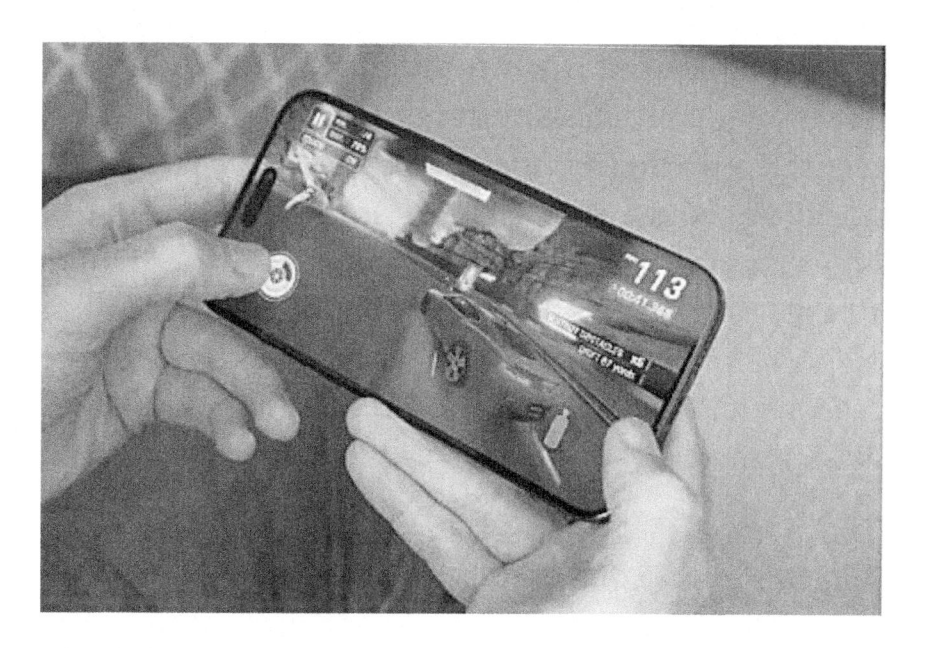

The iPhone 15 Plus, nevertheless, is no slouch. The incredible processing power of the A16 Bionic ensures that not even the most demanding mobile games will cause it any trouble. The primary objective of the A17 Pro is to provide the necessary processing power for full-length console games. We don't think anybody will be disappointed by the iPhone 15 Plus's capabilities in other areas, including computational photography for breathtaking photos or doing hard AI tasks. The added power is wonderful for avid mobile gamers, however.

In this respect, the iPhone 15 Plus excels over the iPhone 15 Pro due to its larger battery capacity.

While the iPhone 15 Pro only achieves 23 and 75 hours of playback time for local films and music, respectively, the iPhone 15 Plus can play videos for up to 26 hours and listen to music for up to 100 hours, according to Apple. The fact that the iPhone 15 Pro may lower the refresh rate of the ProMotion display to save energy likely contributes to the reason that the duration of streaming movies stays at 20 hours.

The iPhone 15 Pro and iPhone 15 Plus both have a half-hour to an hour-and-a-half charging time on a 20-watt charger, but they don't have the rapid charging capabilities seen on many Android phones. The larger battery of the iPhone 15 Plus is the reason for this. Both devices may be charged wirelessly at 15 watts using a MagSafe-certified charger. As with earlier iPhone models, they are limited to 7.5 watts of Qi charging power.

We couldn't make up our minds between the iPhone 15 Plus and the iPhone 15 Pro since they both have excellent battery lives, but the 15 Pro is the performance champ.

iPhone 15 Pro Vs. iPhone 15 Plus: Cameras

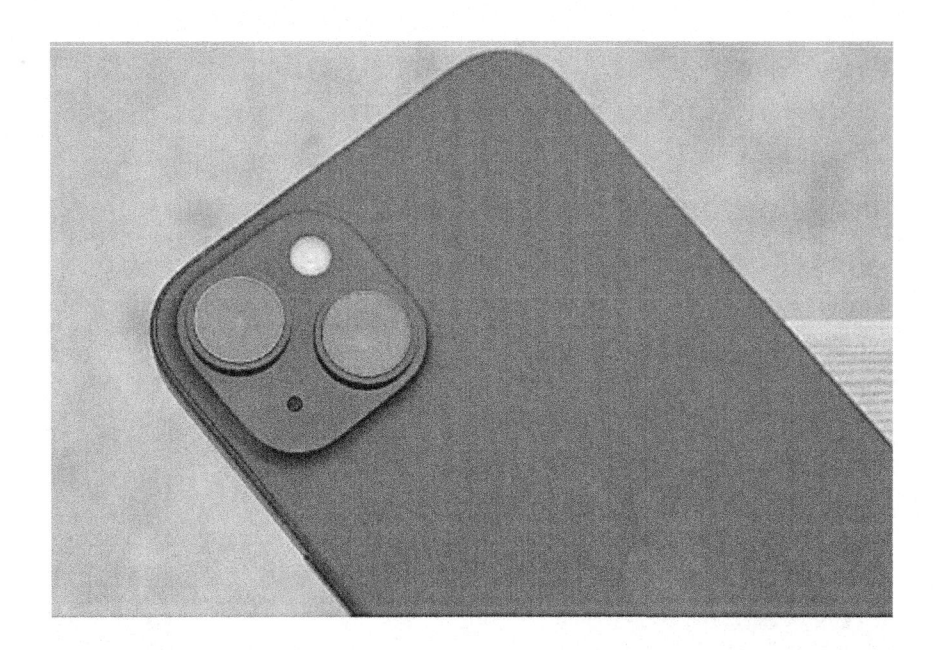

As a matter of thumb, the best camera systems tend to be found in more costly flagship smartphones. That remains true for the iPhone 15 series, however, this year's 15 Plus has better camera hardware than last year's 15 Pro.

Several features are carried over from last year's iPhone 14 Pro, one of which being the high-resolution 48-megapixel camera seen only in the iPhone 15 Plus. Images will be of far better quality, and you'll also get access to a first for Apple's non-Pro iPhones—a simulated 2x optical zoom.

With the new 2x mode, you can make use of the middle 12 megapixels of the 48MP sensor to simulate a third lens, even though there are only two real cameras. This allows for continuous zoom in 4K Cinematic mode and improves portrait mode shooting. "Advanced dual-camera system" is Apple's term for this new feature that sets it apart from earlier models. Even though the iPhone 15 now shoots 24MP shots by default, the 2x zoom only captures 12 megapixels in photographs.

Also, keep in mind that the same technique of cropping the 48MP sensor to generate a virtual optical zoom from the main lens is also used by the iPhone 15 Pro's 2x optical zoom, so this holds. But the iPhone 15 Pro makes up for it with its third camera, which has an optical 3x zoom lens. In addition, the lidar sensor enhances the Portrait mode's depth mapping capabilities, opens up Night mode for portraiture, and speeds up focusing in low-light situations. You may capture images at a macro level and store them in the more complex Apple ProRAW format for later use with editing tools.

Computing photography features including Apple's Photonic Engine, Deep Fusion, and Smart HDR 5 are available on both the iPhone 15 and the iPhone 15 Pro, with the latter boasting a more powerful A17 Pro CPU. If you want your iPhone 15 images to include depth information, you may skip using Portrait Mode since it does it automatically. Applying this effect after the fact will make your photos appear like they were shot in portrait mode.

Superior photo signal processing, including Smart HDR 5, in later iPhone models yields far more vivid and realistic results than the iPhone 14 series' clinically-colored pictures. Even while both the iPhone 15 Plus and the iPhone 15 Pro perform well in brightly lighted areas, the Pro model shines in dimly lit settings. This is mainly because of its adaptive True Tone flash, which is specific to the Pro model, its 3x optical zoom, and its upgraded sensors with stronger optical image stabilization.

Considering the improvements Apple made to its camera system this year, we doubt that anyone other than the most committed photographers would be disappointed with the iPhone 15 Plus, even if the iPhone 15 Pro is better in every aspect.

iPhone 15 Pro Vs. iPhone 15 Plus: Software And Updates

The new Action button on the iPhone 15 Pro is just one example of how iOS 17 is mostly consistent across both the iPhone 15 Plus and the iPhone 15 Pro in terms of the user experience, except for features that are linked to distinguishable physical changes.

The iPhone 15 Pro and iPhone 15 Plus will likely remain compatible with each other for the foreseeable future in terms of software updates. Although Apple doesn't promise any specific update, it has a track record of releasing major software updates for iPhones every five years. Therefore, it's reasonable to assume that all versions of iOS up to and including iOS 22 will be compatible with the iPhone 15 models.

iPhone 15 Pro Vs. iPhone 15 Plus: Special Features

Despite Apple officially standardizing USB-C across all devices with the iPhone 15, the iPhone 15 Pro is designated for faster data transfers. Despite the new connection, the iPhone 15 Plus can only support speeds up to what last year's Lightning port could do.

With a maximum data transmission rate of 10Gbps, the iPhone 15 Pro is compatible with USB 3.1 Gen 2. The iPhone 15 Plus, on the other hand, keeps the 480 Mbps USB 2.0 speeds that have been accessible since the Lightning connector was introduced in 2012, unchanged.

Even while most iPhone users never connect their smartphones to a computer, the iPhone 15 Pro will provide much faster performance for individuals who commonly utilize the old means of uploading media files. The question is how relevant this is in a world like that. You will need to bring your own USB 3.0 cable, however, since the one Apple provides in the box is only compatible with USB 2.0 speeds.

The faster data transfer on the iPhone 15 Pro is mostly attributable to the larger files that the Pro models can capture. The file sizes of ProRAW images (75 MB every shot) or 4K ProRes video (25 GB per minute) at 30 frames per second are much more impressive than 48-megapixel shots or 4K video at 60 frames per second. You may now record 4K ProRes video at 60 fps with the iPhone 15 Pro by using an external drive and the USB-C connection with the correct USB 3 cable. The ability to generate spatial films compatible with Apple's forthcoming Vision Pro mixed-reality headset is on the horizon.

For everyday use, the new Action button on the iPhone 15 Pro stands out more than the old ring/silent switch on the side. Among its many uses, this multi-function button may silence your alarm and launch personalized routines in Apple's Shortcuts app.

iPhone 15 Pro Vs. iPhone 15 Plus: Price And Availability

Apple, along with the majority of carriers and other merchants, offers the iPhone 15 Pro and iPhone 15 Plus.

Starting at $999 for 128GB, the iPhone 15 Pro is available in upgrades to 256GB, 512GB, and 1TB for

$1,099, $1,299, and $1,499, respectively. Natural, blue, white, and black titanium are the available hues.

Prices for the iPhone 15 Plus range from $899 for the 128GB basic model to $1,199 for the 512GB model, with 256GB and 512GB models also available. Black, blue, pink, green, and yellow are the color options.

With its professional-level camera system, lightweight titanium chassis, and very fast A17 Pro CPU, the iPhone 15 Pro offers greater value for your money than the iPhone 15 Plus—yet it's just $100 more expensive.

However, there are cases when it's not as simple as comparing the two specifications. If playing console games or shooting amazing photographs is more important to you than having the largest screen on an iPhone—especially considering that the iPhone 15 Pro Max, which has a screen that is comparable in size, is now $300 more expensive—the iPhone 15 Plus is still a solid choice. The all-new iPhone 15 Plus has an ergonomically perfect and comfortable-to-hold design, a longer battery life, a bigger and more vibrant OLED display, and more. Also, with the dual-lens technology that Apple unveiled in 2019, its camera is the best iPhone camera we've seen so far in 2019.

CHAPTER ONE

THE IPHONE CAMERA BASICS

Discover all the tricks for mastering the iPhone camera. To frame your image, choose a camera mode from the list: Photo, Video, Cinematic, Pano, or Portrait. You may also zoom in or out.

Unveil The Camera

To access Camera, you may perform one of these things:

- Select Camera from the Home Screen of your iPhone.
- The iPhone lock screen may be swung to the left.
- Press and hold the iPhone's camera icon on the lock screen.
- To access the camera, launch Control Center and press the button.

    Just say, "Open Camera," to Siri.

- You have the option to set the Action button on the iPhone 15 Pro and iPhone 15 Pro Max to launch the camera. Refer to The Action button on the iPhone 15 Pro and the iPhone 15 Pro Max may be used and customized.

In the top right corner of your screen, you'll see a green dot that will help you keep track of when the Camera is active.

Take A Photo

Press the volume up or down buttons or the shutter button to snap a picture once you've opened the camera app.

SWITCH BETWEEN CAMERA MODES

When you launch Camera, the default mode is Photo. To capture both static images and moving ones, go to Photo mode. You may switch between several shooting modes by swiping left or right on the screen:

❖ Video

- ❖ Time-Lapse Video.
- ❖ Slow-Motion Video
- ❖ Pano
- ❖ Portrait
- ❖ Cinematic
- ❖ Use a square format for taking pictures.

If you're using an iPhone 11 or later, you may choose between 4:3, 16:9, and Square by tapping the Camera Controls button.

ZOOM IN OR ZOOM OUT

- Utilize the Camera app and the pinch gesture to enlarge or reduce the size of any model.
- For iPhones equipped with dual or triple cameras, you may quickly adjust the magnification level from half ax to five times. Your model will determine the precise figures. Press and hold the zoom buttons while sliding the slider to adjust the zoom level.

HOW TO USE IPHONE CAMERA TO SET UP YOUR SHOT

Use the Camera's editing features to fine-tune your photograph before you snap it.

MODIFY THE EXPOSURE AND FOCUS OF THE CAMERA.

Before taking a picture, the iPhone's camera takes care of focusing and adjusting the exposure. It also uses face recognition to ensure that all of the subjects' faces are properly exposed. Follow these steps if you want to tweak the exposure and focus by hand:

- Switch on the camera.
- Select the focus area and exposure settings automatically by tapping the screen.
- To change the focus area, tap on the desired location.
- The exposure may be adjusted by dragging the Adjust Exposure button, which is located next to the focus area.

Hint: Before taking future photographs, press and hold the focus area until you notice the AE/AF Lock. Then, tap the screen to unlock the settings (manual focus and exposure).

With an iPhone 11 or later, you can lock the exposure for future photographs and adjust it exactly. To change the exposure, press the Exposure button on the Camera Controls button, and then drag the slider. Until you open the Camera again, the exposure will remain locked. Navigate to Settings > Camera > Preserve Settings, and then enable Exposure Adjustment to prevent the exposure setting from being reset every time you use Camera.

Activate Or Deactivate The Flash.

When the light is low, your iPhone camera will automatically switch to using the flash. To adjust the flash by hand before taking a picture, follow these steps:

- To activate or deactivate the automated flash, press the Flash button.
- Select Auto, On, or Off by tapping the Flash button underneath the frame after tapping the Camera Controls button.

Use A Filter To Capture A Picture.

To add some color to your shot, try using a filter.

- Launch the camera app and choose the "Portrait" or "Photo" option.
- Press the Filters button after tapping the Camera Controls button.

- To see how the filters look before you apply them, just swipe left or right underneath the viewer.
- After selecting a filter, press the shutter button to snap the photo.

The Photos app allows you to modify or remove filters from photos.

UTILIZE THE TIMER

To buy yourself more time to acquire the perfect photo, you may use the timer feature on your iPhone's camera.

- Press the Camera Controls button after opening the Camera app.
- Press the Timer button and choose between 3 or 10 seconds.
- The timer may be started by tapping the Shutter button.

TO ENSURE A PERFECTLY LEVEL PHOTO, USE A GRID.

To enable a grid or level on the camera screen, which may assist with composing and straightening your photo, go to Settings > Camera and toggle it on.

Using the editing options in the Photos app, you may further align photos and modify the horizontal and vertical perspective after taking the photo.

CHAPTER TWO

HOW TO MASTER THE CAMERA APP ON IPHONE 15 PRO

Using The Physical Buttons

Many people don't realize this, but the up and down volume keys on an iPhone can take pictures, much like a real shutter button on a camera.

Instead of utilizing the on-screen shutter button, you may swiftly snap a photo by using the up or down volume buttons. This is why some individuals believe that taking images on their phones is easier.

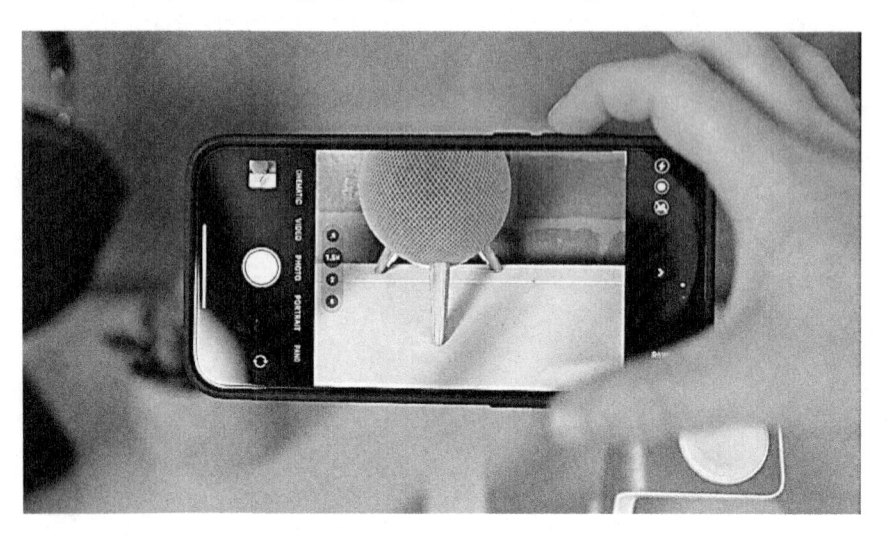

Holding down any button will begin recording. A red timer will appear at the top of the screen and the on-screen shutter button will transform into a red circle to indicate that a video is being filmed.

If you like to take pictures in bursts, you may change the settings to Camera and then use the volume up button to do so.

Holding the volume down button still starts the movie, however holding the volume up button takes a burst of images until you let go of the button.

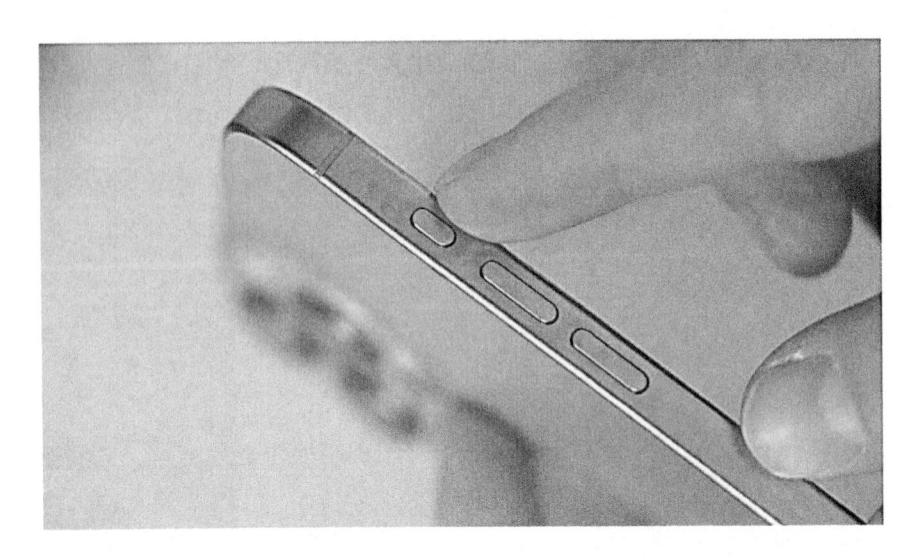

The new customizable Action Button is available on both the pro and regular phones. You may customize this button's behavior in the settings to activate other features, such as the flashlight, or create a voice memo.

While we're discussing cameras, you can access the stock camera app using the presets on the Action Button. Portrait, selfie, video, image, and portrait selfie are just a few of the modes it can flip between.

Launching an external camera app allows for more personalization. Select Shortcut, and then click "open app."

You are free to use whatever third-party program you choose, however, we recommend Halide because it supports new features like zero-lag shutter and forthcoming HDR compatibility.

USING THE ON-SCREEN CONTROLS TO MASTER THE IPHONE 15 PRO CAMERA APP

There are a lot of buttons and sliders in the camera app, and not all of them are easy to see. The shutter button has one of these.

While pressing the shutter button takes a picture, QuickTake isn't as well-known. With QuickTake, you don't even have to switch shooting modes to start taking burst shots or recording video.

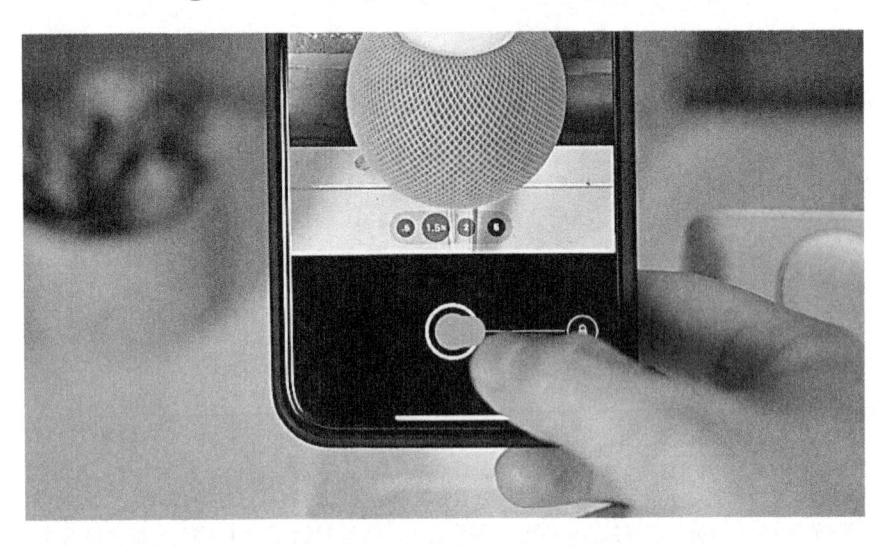

Once you push and hold the shutter button, the video recording procedure starts. When you release the shutter button, the recording will stop.

Sliding the button to the right will lock you into video mode, so you won't have to keep hitting the shutter button when shooting a QuickTake movie.

Apple incorporated a cute animation where the red square indicating the video recording turns into a red circle as you move it. In case you were wondering, yes, you can still take a picture by pressing that circle while recording the video.

The same holds for starting burst shots: press and hold the shutter button, then swiftly drag to the left. Your burst photographs will cease as soon as you let go of the shutter.

THE IPHONE 15 PRO AND 15 PRO MAX'S ZOOM LEVELS

In terms of ultra-wide cameras, the iPhone 15 Pro and 15 Pro Max share two main and one secondary setup. A wide-angle shot is captured by the secondary camera, while the main camera acts as a 1X zoom. Make five separate zooms.

The telephoto lens on the iPhone 15 Pro Max offers 5X optical zoom, up from 3X on the iPhone 15 Pro.

Managing them is a piece of cake. On the screen, you'll see four buttons that may be used for navigation. Zoom settings of 5X, 1X, 2X and 3X/5X are available.

An additional feature of the primary camera allows you to change the main zoom to 1.2X or 1.5X by touching the 1X button. Here we have focal lengths of 24mm, 28mm, and 35mm.

You may make one of them the default for that Main camera by returning to the camera settings.

You may access a granular adjustment wheel by tapping and holding any of the zoom levels, and then swiping left or right. The ability to precisely regulate the amount of zoom is far more satisfying than the previous method of attempting to squeeze the screen.

You can easily fine-tune your shot with only one hand. When you release your grip on the screen, the wheel will disappear automatically, or you may swipe it away.

GETTING THE MOST OUT OF YOUR IPHONE 15 PRO'S CAMERA APP: EXTRA FEATURES, OPTIONS, AND CONTROLS

You may switch between various camera modes with a simple swipe of the left or right finger while you're recording video or stills. There are a variety of picture settings to choose from, including portrait, panoramic, cinematic, and slo-mo for video.

To focus an image, press anywhere on the screen; to lock the exposure, hold down the shutter button. You may instantly change the exposure by tapping the subject and dragging your finger up and down.

After you've mastered the fundamentals, we may continue to the more complex controls. More than one of those buttons sits above the camera app's main UI.

The program's main interface includes icons for frequently used functions, such as the shared library, night mode, and flash, which are situated there. The Live Photos toggle is located on the right side of the screen.

By touching the center caret, you may reach the settings tray, which is situated at the bottom of the program, just above the shutter button. Some tools grant you more power, even when they seem like copies from above.

At first, you'll see the flash icon. This tray, in contrast to the two preceding ones, lets you choose between auto, on, and off.

Next to it is the night mode toggle; however, unlike the top, this one also lets you choose the shutter time. Depending on the lighting and your hand's stability, it will automatically alter the length.

The shutter will only open for three seconds if you're not perfectly still, but it may remain open for up to thirty seconds when your phone is mounted on a tripod.

Just as with Live Photos, you can toggle it between on, auto, and off. Our favorite feature of Life Photos is their ability to record both the subject and the environment, as well as post-shot animations.

Stacks of squares indicate that Photographic Styles is the item next in line. Standard, rich, lively, warm, and cold are the five available styles.

Tone and warmth controls allow you to personalize each of them. To return to the default, you may use the reset button for each style.

The remaining parameters include an aspect ratio (4:3, 1:1, and 16:9), exposure correction, a timer, filters, and a shared library.

HOW TO MASTER THE CAMERA APP ON IPHONE 15 PRO- EXTRA SHOOTING MODES

You may activate additional modes for both images and movies in addition to the usual ones. We touched on night mode briefly up there; it turns on automatically. However, there are a few more to go over.

To get up close and personal with your subjects, switch to macro mode and use the ultra-wide lens. It works similarly to night mode in that it is activated automatically if the camera detects a subject near the phone.

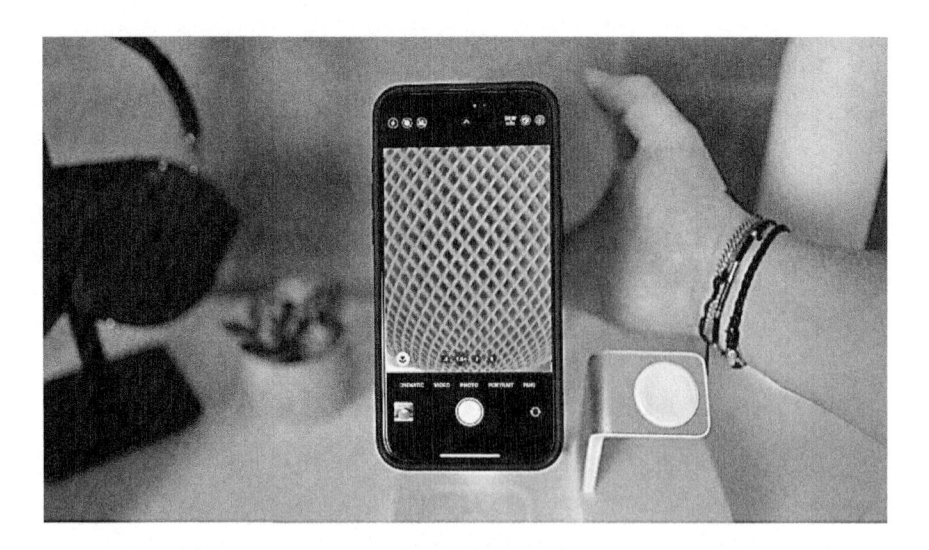

When a little flower symbol shows up in the bottom-left corner of the UI, it means it is in macro mode. You can disable macro mode in the Camera app's settings by pressing the flower symbol, and it's also optional.

So now we're in portrait mode. The latest iPhones make it possible to take portraits without constantly switching to portrait mode.

You may be surprised to hear that the Camera app takes depth data for portrait shots whenever it recognizes an on-screen human, dog, or cat. When this occurs, a stylized f will appear in the bottom right corner, allowing you to modify the blur level.

When taking a regular Live Photo with depth data, you'll have the option to choose between the two formats after the fact.

With the ability to capture your child's or pet's every action as a Live Photo or to achieve a styled portrait style, you have the "best of both worlds" in every shot.

However, the Camera app's portrait mode is still available, so you can still use it to capture images of objects, animals, or cocktails.

When recording video, use the action mode to steady very unsteady footage. To activate it when in video mode, touch the running symbol.

Media Playback On The iPhone 15 Pro And iPhone 15 Pro Max

While recording video, you have the option to choose between two modes: slo-mo, which records at a maximum of 240 FPS, and cinematic.

More or less, cinematic mode is a portrait mode for video. While blurring the backdrop, it follows your topic, ensuring that it remains sharp.

You may change the focus after the event or shift it to other parts of the screen. It was enhanced with the iPhone 15 series so that it could record at 24, 35, or 30 fps.

Professionals and individuals seeking more control have the choice to film in ProRes with HDR, SDR, or log color. When a USB-C connection is made, video may be recorded straight to an external solid-state drive.

How To Master The Camera App on iPhone 15 Pro - Other Settings

As if that weren't enough, the Camera app also has some more advanced options to think about.

You have the option to enable RAW mode for your images. By shooting in RAW, users may enhance their images by bringing out more details in the shadows and highlights.

You can find Apple's RAW image choices under the "Pro Default" settings. Users may choose between 12MP ProRAW photos, 48MP ProRAW Max, or large 48MP JPEG images called JPEG Max.

Instead of the compressed 12MP that was previously accessible, the new 24MP option lets users record standard images shot with the main lens.

You have the option to enable or disable the HDR function for videos. Editing using HDR or Dolby Vision in Final Cut Pro or another tool could be more difficult, but the result will be worth it.

A new feature in the camera app in iOS 17 makes it easier to keep your subject level while taking pictures or movies. A little line appears on the screen as a result of this function.

CHAPTER THREE

HOW TO SET PHOTOGRAPHIC STYLES ON IPHONE CAMERA

If you own an iPhone, you may use Photographic Styles to automatically enhance your photos to perfection.

While many photographers look forward to spending several hours in top-tier editing software perfecting their camera shots, it's not uncommon to feel the complete reverse. Moreover, it's reasonable to believe that editing images on an iPhone isn't worth the effort, considering how often people use their phones for casual photo taking.

Imagine instead if you could automatically make adjustments to your photographs as you shoot them. if way, you'd never have to touch up those images by hand again! Photographic Styles is useful for that. In a nutshell, this obscure iPhone camera feature lets you apply effects to your shots in real-time. It can enhance the contrast, brightness, warmth, and coolness of your photographs. Once you've established a Photographic Style, your phone may automatically apply that appearance whenever you wish it.

HOW TO SET PHOTOGRAPHIC STYLES ON IPHONE

1. To access the three squares icon in the Camera app, launch it, then slide up when in Photo mode.

2. To see the effects of each Photographic Style on your photograph, swipe left to browse them.

3. To adjust the warmth and tone of a selected photographic style, hit the sliders and then utilize the expanded sliders.

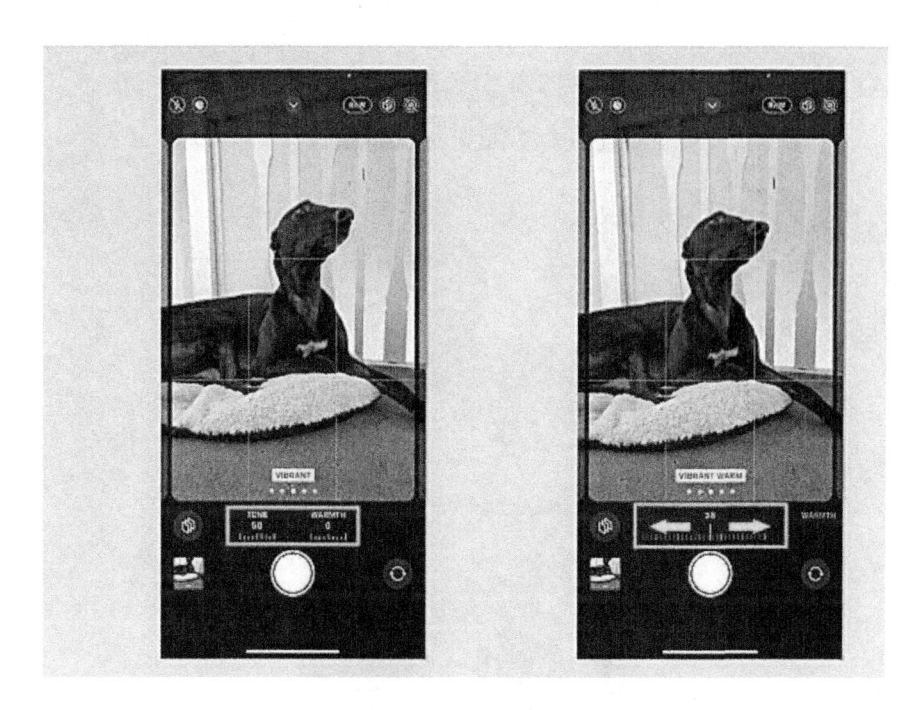

4. To utilize the Photographic Style, just snap a shot when you're pleased.

5. The Settings menu also provides access to the different Photographic Styles, so you may learn more about their functions there. This approach allows you to select a photographic style and provides a short explanation of its impact. To access the photographic styles, launch the Settings app, then go to Camera.

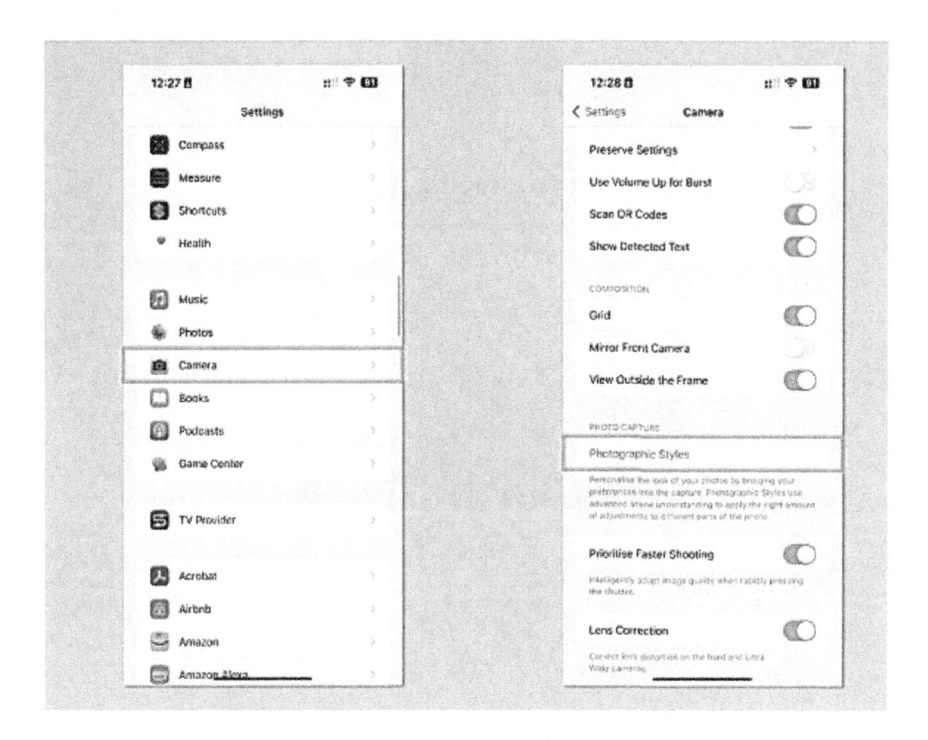

6. To examine how each style affects a picture, swipe through them. Then, press "Use "Style" to apply a style.

Your camera will remember the Photographic Style you select until you return it to Standard; there's no need to save it as a preserved preset. Because you can't erase or eliminate the impact of these Styles, which limits your options in post-production, be sure you reset the camera to Standard if you want to edit the photographs afterward.

HOW TO TAKE LIVE PHOTOS

To take a Live Photo, you may record 1.5 seconds of video and audio both before and after you press the shutter button. Along with a 12-megapixel static JPEG photo, it also offers a Live Photo that lasts three seconds.

If you own an iPhone 7/7 Plus, iPhone SE, or iPhone 6s/6s Plus, you can snap live photographs using their camera app.

The process of taking a live photo is as follows:

- Start by opening the camera app.
- To activate Live Photos, touch the symbol that looks like a camera in the upper center of the screen.
- Press the white shutter button.

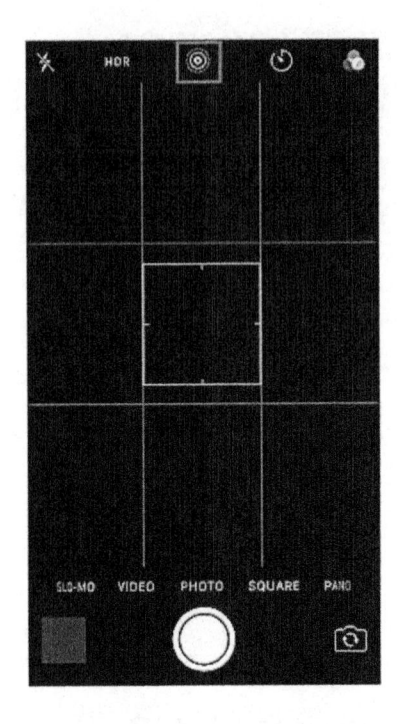

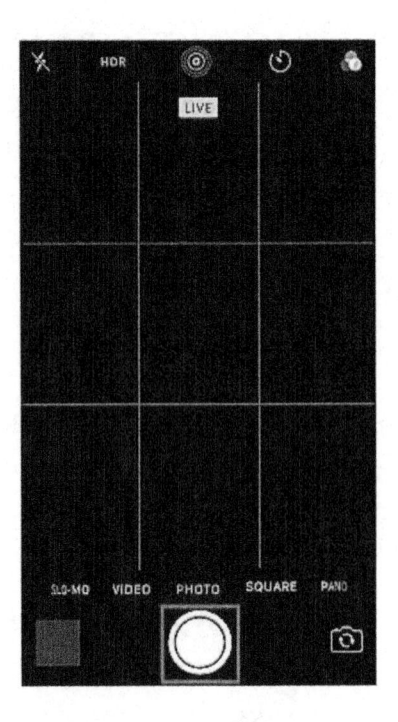

HOW TO VIEW AND EDIT LIVE PHOTO

You can find your captured Live Photos in the Photos app. The Photos app allows you to edit Live Photos in the same way you edit regular still photos.

To see an Up-Current Image:

To launch Live Photo, tap on a thumbnail of a picture. To make the picture move, push and hold the screen firmly.

To Make Changes to Real-Time Images:

- Open a Live Photo and then touch the Edit icon.
- Modify a live photo using the editing tools that will emerge.

Cropping, rotating, applying filters, and adjusting lighting and colors are all possible with these tools.

7. Hit done to save your changes when you're done altering your Live Photo.

RESTORE THE ORIGINAL LIVE PHOTO.

You always have the option to return to the original Live Photo if you change your mind about the edits you made.

STATIC IMAGE CONVERSION FROM LIVE PHOTO

While viewing a Live Photo, press the Edit icon. Then, tap the blue Live Photos sign to convert it to a still image. You can tell when a photo is no longer a Live Photo because the icon becomes white. Validation is as easy as clicking the "Done" button.

Just like that, you may always go back to the default Live Photo.

HOW TO SHARE LIVE PHOTOS

You may communicate or share a significant moment with your loved ones after capturing and editing a Live Photo. With iMessage, AirDrop, or the iCloud Photo Library, you can easily transfer Live Photos to any other iOS device.

- Go to the bottom left of your screen and tap the Share button. This will allow you to share Live Photos.

    Press Live in the top left corner to share the still image instead of the live one.

- Choose a sharing method, such as iMessage or Airdrop, if you like.

For easy identification, Live Photos are tagged as such.

A growing number of social networking sites will likely add support for Live Photos shortly, joining Facebook and Tumble in this capability.

HOW TO TURN OFF LIVE PHOTOS TEMPORARILY

For your next shoot, follow these steps to disable Live Photos. It will automatically turn back on for subsequent shots.

1. Open the Camera app and locate the Live Photos target.

The Live Photos animated yellow bullseye symbol and the arrow icon that controls different camera settings can be seen at the top right and top center of your screen, respectively, once you activate the Camera app.

2. Press down on the target.

You will notice a brief note showing the change in status—this will switch off the Live Photos capability. The function is disabled when a white bullseye button is slashed across the top.

HOW TO DISABLE LIVE PHOTOS

Here are the procedures to fully disable Live Photos. If you want to enable Live Photos again, you can simply follow these procedures and undo the adjustments later on.

- To begin, go to the Settings menu.
- Next, choose the camera icon.

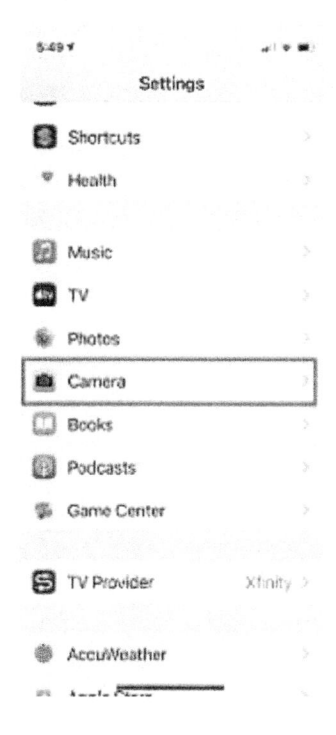

- Enable Live Photos by clicking the Preserve Settings button.

THINGS TO KNOW BEFORE DISABLING LIVE PHOTOS

Any further shots will be regular stills once you disable Live Photos, but any Live Photos you've already taken will stay in your Camera Roll.

- In the Camera app, you can also access Live Photos by tapping the center top arrow. It provides a wide array of settings for the camera's many features, including video, flash, exposure, aspect ratio, timer, and Live Photos.

- You can toggle the Live Photos feature on and off, or set it to auto-play whenever you want by tapping the Live Photos button.

CHAPTER FOUR

HOW TO TAKE PORTRAITS WITH YOUR IPHONE CAMERA

You may get a stunning blurring of the foreground and background with a depth-of-field effect using the Camera on models that support Portrait mode. This effect works with subjects (people, pets, objects, etc.) while keeping them crisp. In addition, you have the option to add and modify various lighting effects to your photos.

TAKE A PORTRAIT IN PORTRAIT MODE

1. Go to the Camera app and choose Portrait mode.
2. In the yellow portrait box, frame your subject by following the onscreen instructions if asked to do so.

To toggle between multiple zoom choices, press 1x, 2x, or 3x on compatible models.

The ability to pinch the screen to zoom in and out is available in iPhone 15 models.

3. To choose a lighting effect, just drag the Portrait Lighting control:
    - The lighting is natural, and the subject's face stands out against the background's softness.
    - The shot has a clean, studio-lit appearance, and the subject's face is well-lit.
    - Contour Light: The face's highlights and lowlights create striking shadows.
    - Spotlights illuminate the face against a pitch-black stage backdrop.
    - Similar to Stage Light, but with a traditional black-and-white picture. This effect is called Stage Light Mono.
    - A grayscale subject set against a white backdrop is achieved using High-Key Light Mono.
4. For the shutter button to be pressed, press it.

If you're not happy with the results of the portrait mode, you may undo the effects after the photo. By opening the photo, going to Edit, and finally clicking

Portrait in the Photos app, you may activate or deactivate the Portrait effect.

Note: On some models, Night mode is activated while taking portraits in low light using the wide (1x) lens. You may learn more about how to utilize Night mode by viewing the "Take Night mode photos" section.

Note: You may edit your photos with various photography effects when you shoot in Portrait mode.

Note: The only method to access Stage Light, Stage Light Mono, and High-Key Light Mono on the iPhone XR is via the front-facing camera.

ADJUST DEPTH CONTROL IN PORTRAIT MODE

For more or less blurred backgrounds in your pictures, use the Depth Control slider.

- Launch Camera, toggle to Portrait mode, and position your subject accordingly.
- In the upper right corner of the screen, you should see the Depth Adjustment button. Tap on it.
Just below the picture, you can see the Depth Control slider.

- You may change the effect's intensity by using the slider.
- For the shutter button to be pressed, press it.

The Photos app's Depth Control slider allows you to fine-tune the blur effect of the backdrop after you've taken a portrait.

MODIFY THE LIGHTING FOR A PORTRAIT WHILE IN PORTRAIT MODE

Virtually change the angle and brightness of the Portrait Lighting to bring out more defined eyes or soften wrinkles and blemishes.

- To pick a lighting effect, open Camera, go to Portrait mode, then drag the Portrait Lighting control.
- On top of the screen, you should see the Portrait Control button; tap on it.
  Just below the frame, you can find the Portrait Lighting slider.
- You may change the effect's intensity by using the slider.
- For the shutter button to be pressed, press it.

You may adjust the Portrait Lighting settings in the Photos app after taking the shot.

TAKE A PORTRAIT IN PHOTO MODE

When shooting in Photo mode on iPhone 15 models, you have the option to blur the backdrop and add the portrait effect.

Tap to turn portrait effects on and off in Photo mode.

1. Shutter Release.

    The Depth button will show at the bottom of the viewfinder on your iPhone when it detects a human, dog, or cat.

Note: If you want to add a portrait effect to your images after the fact, you can do so in the images app since your iPhone records depth information whenever the Depth button shows up when shooting in Photo mode.

2. If you're not seeing the Depth button, try tapping an object in the viewfinder to bring it into focus. Simply tapping on a new topic in the viewfinder will shift the portrait's focal point.
3. To capture a picture with the portrait effect, press the Depth button and then the Shutter button.

Note: When you shoot a portrait in Photo mode, you have the option to apply photographic styles.

HOW TO USE THE IPHONE TO EDIT PORTRAITS

You may edit your portraits' lighting, focus, and depth of field in the Photos app. On compatible models, you may also use the Photo mode to add portrait effects to your images.

MODIFY THE LIGHTING EFFECT FOR PORTRAITS

You can add, modify, or delete the Portrait Lighting effects in portraits on models that support it.

1. To see a portrait on full screen, touch on it, and then hit Edit.

87

2. To choose a lighting effect, use the Depth Adjustment button and then drag the Portrait Lighting control.
   - The lighting is natural, and the subject's face stands out against the background's softness.
   - The shot has a clean, studio-lit appearance, and the subject's face is well-lit.
   - Contour Light: The face's highlights and lowlights create striking shadows.
   - Spotlights illuminate the face against a pitch-black stage backdrop.
   - Like Stage Light, but with a traditional black-and-white picture. This effect is called Stage Light Mono.
   - On compatible devices, High-Key Light Mono will produce a monochrome subject on a white backdrop.

Note: The front-facing camera on the iPhone XR is the only one that can use Natural Light, Studio Light, and Contour Light modes.

3. Light intensity may be adjusted by dragging the slider to the left or right.
4. To save your changes, tap Done.

After saving Portrait Lighting, you may return to the original lighting by tapping Edit and then Revert.

Important: Go to the top of the screen and press on Portrait to disable Portrait Lighting.

MODIFY PORTRAIT DEPTH CONTROL

To control the amount of blurring the backdrop in your portraits, use the Depth Control slider (for models that allow it).

1. To see a portrait on full screen, touch on it, and then hit Edit.
2. To adjust the amount of blurring applied to the backdrop, just drag the Depth Control slider.

   The photo's initial depth value is shown by a white dot.

3. To save your changes, tap Done.

ADJUST A PORTRAIT'S FOCAL LENGTH

By adjusting the focal point, you may alter the topic of a portrait. The background blur is automatically adjusted to make the selected subject seem crisp and in focus as soon as you pick it. Verify that the newly introduced topic is not too distant or hazy.

- Launch the iPhone's Photos app.
- To see a portrait on full screen, touch on it, and then hit Edit.
- Alter the photo's focal point or topic by tapping on it.
- Press the Finish button.

Important: This feature is only accessible on iPhone 13 and later devices with iOS 16 or later when taking a portrait.

USE THE PORTRAIT FILTER ON IMAGES CAPTURED IN THE CAMERA'S PICTURE MODE.

Taken in Photo mode, portraits of people, dogs, or cats may be turned into beautiful images in the Photos app on iPhone 15 models.

- Launch the iPhone's Photos app.
- Select an image to see it on full screen while shooting in Photo mode, and then touch Edit.
- To access portrait effects, go to the top of the screen and touch Portrait, then hit the Depth Adjustment button.
- The slider for Depth Control allows you to adjust the blurring of the portrait's backdrop.
- Press the Finish button.

Once you've opened the picture, go to Edit > Revert to remove the portrait effects.

Note: When shooting in Photo mode and applying the portrait effect, you will not be able to use any of the Live Photo effects. You may see the Live Photo or add an effect to it without the portrait mode by tapping Live.

CHAPTER FIVE

HOW TO TAKE PANORAMA PHOTOS WITH IPHONE

At its most fundamental, panoramic pictures record a wide-angle perspective of an object or scene. This perspective is lengthier and more broad than the typical wide-angle image.

There are mainly two ways to take panoramas. If you want a panoramic view, the best option is to use a specialized camera. You may also just use a regular camera and pan around to capture various parts of the landscape.

The term "panning" describes the movement of the camera from a still image to a moving one. If you follow these steps, you can use your iPhone to take panoramic photos.

How does one go about taking a panoramic shot using an Apple iPhone? Start by going to your iPhone's camera app and looking for the Pano option toward the bottom of the screen. For those using Pano mode, a little line and an arrow may be seen in the lower-left corner of the screen.

Hold the arrow in the center of the line while you move the phone horizontally after pressing the shutter button. Slowly go forward. You won't even need to move a muscle thanks to the automatic picture-taking and stitching.

METHODS FOR MAINTAINING A STABLE IPHONE

iPhone panoramas are many photos stitched together to form a single lengthy shot. A warped or crooked shot will result from excessive movement during panning.

Maintaining a hand-to-chest ratio can help your pano photo come out sharp. You have a higher chance of maintaining a level arrow trajectory if you move as little as possible.

Stay away from holding it so near that you can't see the screen, however. Be very careful not to take your gaze off the arrow. It's the only way to guarantee that your shot will be level.

Think about investing in a tripod if you're not confident with your hand-holding abilities. Take your selfie stick and attach it to the tripod by removing the phone holder. Next, snap your gadget onto it and fire away as if it were in your hand.

To slide your iPhone from side to side, loosen the pan-locking knob. Tighten the knob that locks the tilt simultaneously. By doing so, you may avoid having your picture distorted due to your phone inadvertently going up or down.

THE IMPORTANCE OF HOME PRACTICE FOR IPHONE PANORAMAS

Panoramas shot with an iPhone are a breeze. However, it is recommended to practice panning inside first, before venturing outside. You won't have to fiddle with your phone and miss shots when the time arrives.

The goal of the game is to maintain control of the arrow as it moves down the yellow line on the screen. Start by snapping a picture using your phone's camera. The next time you use a tripod, give it a go. Assuming you can master the motion and maintain proper alignment, you should be good to go.

For the steadiest images, a tripod is recommended to be used with your phone. You can't use it constantly, however. For example, several popular tourist locations have strict policies against the use of tripods.

Also, there are instances when you just don't have room for any additional gear. It's in situations like this that being able to capture panoramas handed comes in handy.

METHODS FOR CREATING PANORAMAS ON AN IPHONE

Composing panorama photographs on an iPhone is another ability that might be useful.

Your screen cannot show the full length of a panoramic photo. Therefore, decide beforehand how much of the scene you want to record.

First things first, take stock of your environment and mark out any potential shooting locations. Pick landmarks to indicate the beginning and ending points of your panorama after you've located a suitable spot.

Before you snap the shot, try to capture the whole picture with a single swipe of your phone's screen. Taking a few practice shots is also helpful.

You may adjust the composition and make sure the parts you want to be in the shot by doing this.

Simply hit the iPhone camera shutter button where you would want the panorama to terminate to restrict its length. At the duration you choose, your phone will cease capturing the pano photo.

At the end of the process, you may clip the frame automatically by swiveling your smartphone to the left.

HOW TO BREAK COMPOSITION RULES FOR MORE CREATIVE PHOTOS

Do you recall the many stages needed to capture the ideal panorama on an iPhone? Forget about following them if you so choose. Do you have any idea what you could receive?

Just do it and observe what happens when you disregard compositional norms.

To begin, pan the screen by gently raising and lowering your phone. When you do this, the objects in your photograph will likely get warped. However, this method is worth trying if you want psychedelic effects.

The next time you take a panoramic, instead of avoiding moving subjects, try catching them. Put aside any concerns about how it will look in your photo. Take a picture and be surprised.

Your shot might take on a more fascinating and distinctive appearance with warped and stretched items.

Cloning individuals into your images is another option to consider. To begin the picture, have a buddy stand at the spot you've chosen. Have them sprint behind you and stand where you'd want the panorama to terminate as you move your phone from side to side. When you're done filming, your companion will show up at the beginning and the conclusion of the pano.

WHY YOU SHOULD AVOID MOVING OBJECTS

Do you recall how your phone could snap many shots and merge them into one? An item will seem stretched and warped if it is in motion while the camera is taking the picture. This indicates that areas with plenty of people and cars should be avoided.

One major limitation of iPhone panoramas is their inability to capture movement. However, it doesn't rule out any possible solutions.

Visiting when the weather is less hot and muggy is the simplest option. Sunrise and sunset are ideal shooting periods. You may take panoramic pictures without worrying about anyone obstructing them since most people are still in bed.

In addition to that, you will get the opportunity to see the breathtaking golden hourlight. Shifting your viewpoint is another strategy. To sidestep crowded spots, just tilt your phone vertically, horizontally, or even laterally.

HOW TO TAKE A SELFIE ON IPHONE CAMERA

To snap your very first selfie with your iPhone, just follow these simple instructions.

1. On the home screen of your iPhone, find the Camera icon.
2. A front-facing camera may be selected by tapping the Switch Camera icon.

3. Choose from Portrait and Photo. For more artistic selfies, try using the Portrait Lighting feature or the Portrait mode, which both blur the backdrop.
    - To adjust the viewing angle in the Photo mode, press and hold the white arrows with two heads.
    - Click the shutter button in Portrait mode when the Depth Effect box becomes yellow.
4. To capture a selfie, just position your face and click the shutter button or both volume buttons. When the phone gets too near to your face, the camera app will let you know to take a step back.
5. The Photos app is where your iPhone stores the selfie.

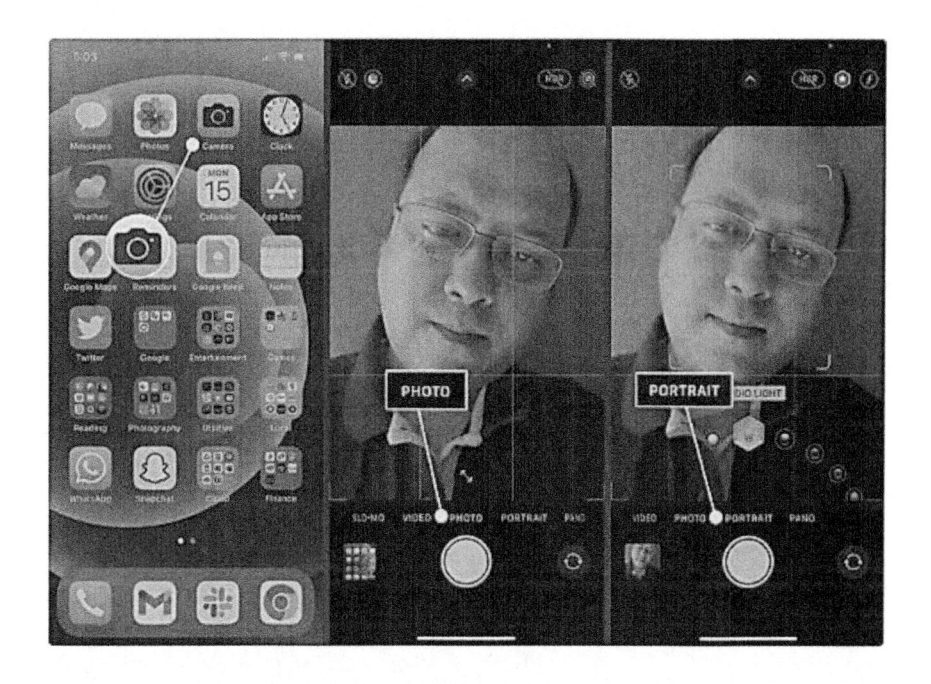

Tip: Go to Settings > Enable Mirror Front Camera on iPhone XS, iPhone XR, and later models to shoot a selfie that appears just like the one you see when you look at the front-facing camera. Go to Photos > Mirror Front Photos on the iPhone X and before.

IMPROVING YOUR SELFIES WITH THE IPHONE CAMERA APP

Initiating, the built-in iPhone camera app may seem to be lacking in features. Unfortunately, a plethora of tools for improving your selfie are hidden within. So, to help you shoot the ideal selfie, we've compiled a list of the top ones:

- For more creative selfies, try using one of the six Portrait lighting options.
- You may blur the backdrop and bring the emphasis on your face by adjusting the Depth-of-Field, which is the focal length slider.
- Pose for an automated selfie by using the three- or ten-second timed delay.

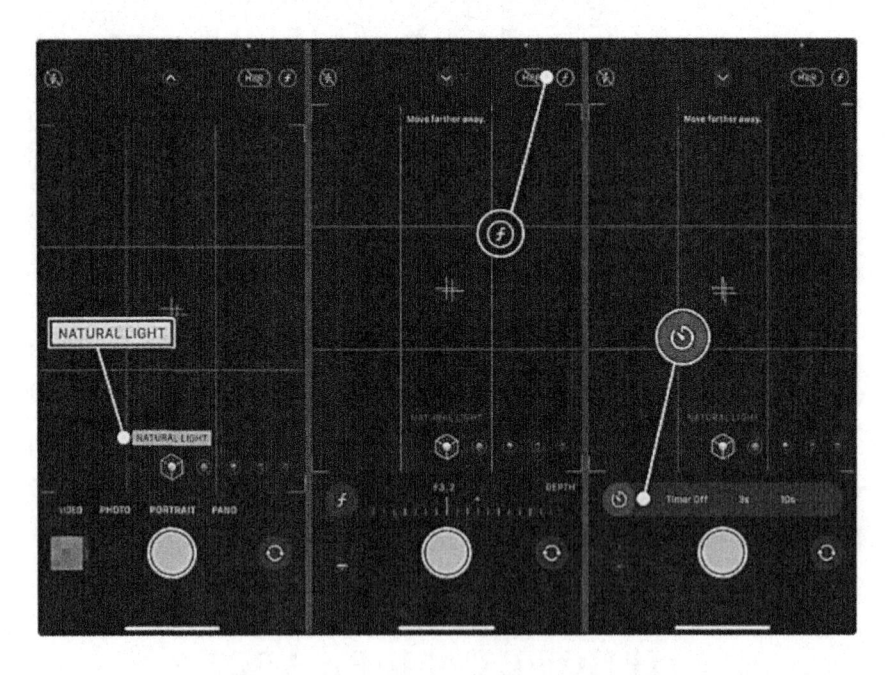

- In both Portrait and Photo modes, you may manually control the amount of light that hits the face by using the Exposure slider.
- For selfies you want to share on social media, choose the Square picture option in the picture mode.

- To enhance low-light selfies, turn on the flash (in both Portrait and Photo mode).

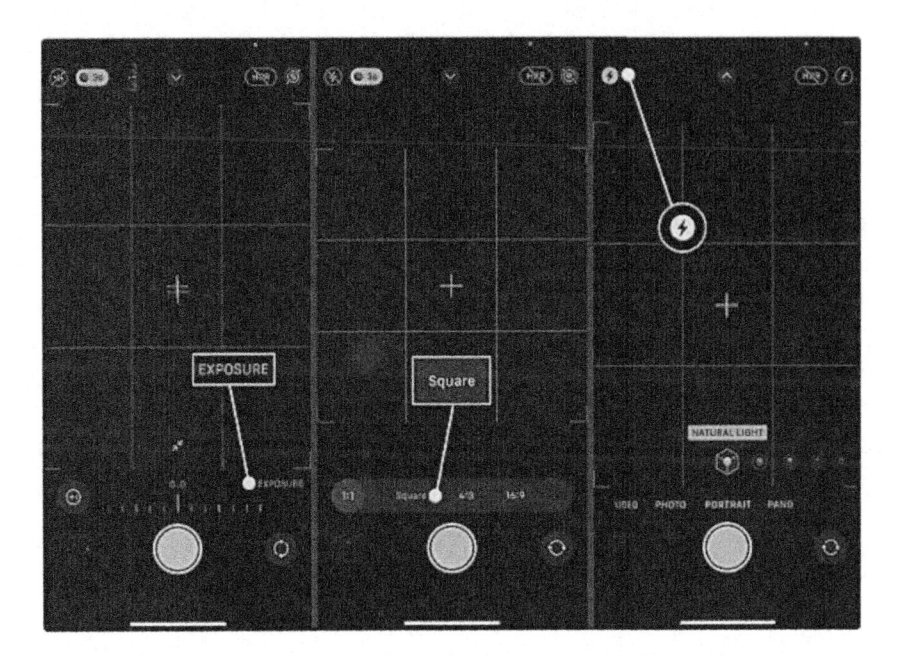

Note: The built-in lens correction feature of the iPhone 12 and 13 uses an algorithm to enhance the realism of photos. To experiment with the results, you may deactivate the feature by heading to Settings > Camera > Turn off Lens Correction.

HOW TO TAKE A GOOD SELFIE

An acronym, such as LCP (Lighting, Composition, and Posing), might serve as a helpful reminder of the fundamental guidelines for taking selfies. You could fill a book with advice on how to shoot great selfies, but these are the bare minimum.

Maintain Your iPhone's Camera Lens

Avoid taking selfies in low light or with visible dust grains by keeping the lens of your camera clean and free of stains. Before taking a picture, wipe the glass with a lint-free, gentle cloth.

Locate An Appropriate Background

The perfect backdrop will eliminate any unnecessary elements, allowing the viewer to concentrate on your face. Pick an uncluttered spot and use a backdrop color that goes well with your outfit for the selfie.

Get The Light From The Sun

Selfies are best taken in diffused, gentle natural light. The morning and evening are ideal times to shoot pictures since the light is warmer and more flattering. Another option is to stand next to a window, which will let the light bounce off the walls and soften the brightness.

Turn Towards The Light Source

Avoid casting unflattering shadows by keeping your back to the light at all times. Lights positioned low on the ground will cast a shadow behind the eyes and chin, so it's preferable to keep them at arm's length for optimal effects.

Make Better Compositions By Making Use Of The Grid

Navigating to Settings > Camera > Composition > Grid on an iPhone will enable the Rule of Thirds Grid. Make sure your face is positioned so that the four lines overlap at the junction for the ideal selfie angle. By doing so, your best characteristics will stand out.

Try Out The Rearview Mirror

Finding the sweet spot for your selfie's focus length is essential. The back cameras of some iPhone Pro models are also more powerful than others. Use the timer to try out different still selfie or action pose options, even if the back camera has a hard time focusing.

To Minimize Camera Shake, Wear Earphones Or Earbuds.

Camera wobble may be caused by tapping the screen or using the side button to shutter. Alternatively, tap the up or down volume button on the headphones to take a selfie when the iPhone is in portrait mode and on a flat surface.

CHAPTER SIX

HOW TO TAKE MACRO PHOTOS AND VIDEOS WITH YOUR IPHONE CAMERA

To get macro shots—beautiful, crisp close-ups—on compatible models, the Camera employs the Ultra Wide camera. You can capture macro images, Live Photos, and slow-motion or time-lapse films.

DOCUMENT THE SUBJECT WITH A CLOSE-UP SHOT OR VIDEO

- Launch the iPhone Camera app and choose between the Photo and Video modes.
- Approach the object up close, within two cm at the most. You won't even have to touch the button to switch to the Ultra Wide lens.
- Use the shutter button to snap a picture, or press and hold the record button to begin and end the video recording.

TAKE A MACRO SLOW-MOTION OR TIME-LAPSE VIDEO

- Get your iPhone's Camera app and go to the Slo-mo or Time-lapse settings.

- Press the 5x button to activate the Ultra Wide camera, and then approach the subject up close.
- To begin and end the recording, just tap the Record button.

CONTROL AUTOMATIC MACRO SWITCHING

When you want to take macro shots or movies, you may set the camera to automatically switch to the Ultra Wide lens.

- Launch the iPhone camera app and approach the topic closely.

    The Auto Macro On button will show up on the screen as soon as you approach your subject at a macro distance.

- To disable automatic macro switching, tap the Auto Macro On button.

    Advice: Press or backspace the screen if the image or video becomes fuzzy. Press 5x to activate the Ultra Wide lens.

- To restore automatic macro switching, press the Auto Macro Off button.

Navigate to Settings > Camera > Macro Control to disable the feature that automatically switches to the Ultra Wide camera for macro shots and movies.

Go to Settings > Camera > Preserve Settings, and then enable Macro Control if you like to save your Macro Control option across camera sessions.

HOW TO USE NIGHT MODE CAMERA ON IPHONE

Note: Night mode is a feature that all iPhones, beginning with the 11, have. Night mode portraits are exclusive to the Pro models (iPhone 12 Pro and after), whereas night mode selfies are accessible on all iPhone 12 models and later.

1. Launch the Camera app and toggle on the Night mode.

To use the photo mode, launch your phone's camera app and swipe to it.

The moon symbol, which is located in the upper left corner next to the flash icon, will change yellow to indicate that Night mode has been activated when the lens detects low-light circumstances.

Night mode is disabled if the light bulb symbol isn't yellow. This is because the camera isn't able to identify low-light conditions. Also, if it's crossed out, Night mode is off, so it won't turn on regardless of how dim the light is. In this situation, you may activate Night mode by tapping on its icon.

2. Snatch up and keep still

When you're ready, press and hold the shutter button to take a picture. The key is to remain still; we'll explain why in a little.

3. Set the duration of the night mode's capture.

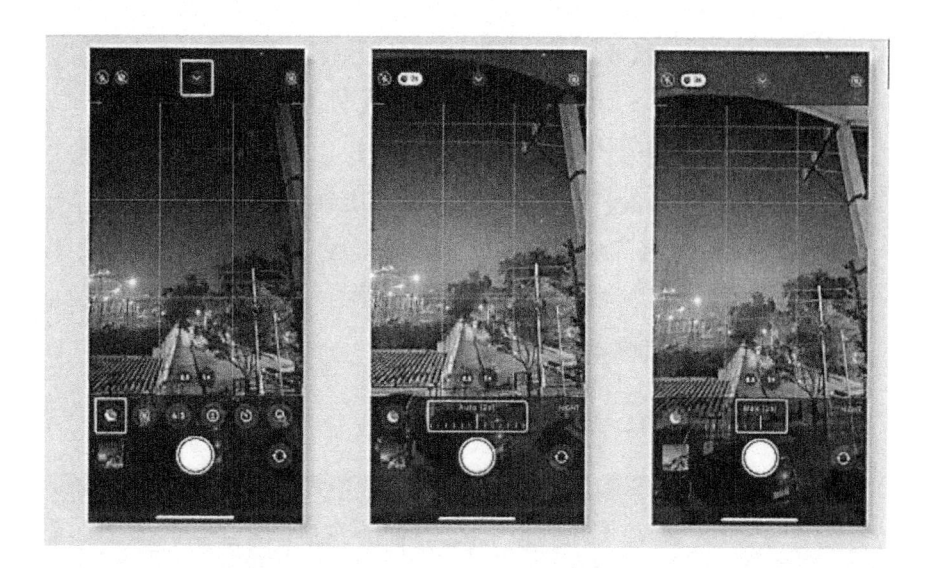

To access the Camera settings, slide up on the picture preview or hit the arrow at the top (just under the notch) if the automated Night mode doesn't brighten the image sufficiently.

To set the time for when the photo is captured, tap the moon symbol in the settings. The slider is located above the shutter button; the maximum duration may be anywhere from one second to thirty seconds, depending on the surrounding light. You may get a brighter picture by extending the capture duration.

After you've adjusted the slider, press the shutter button and hold firm until the capture is finished.

5 TIPS FOR GETTING THE BEST NIGHT MODE SHOTS

If you own an iPhone, here are some pointers on how to maximize the use of Night mode. However, if you're serious about improving your low-light photography, we suggest splurging on a top mirrorless camera.

1. Keep The Phone Steady

The most crucial aspect is to remain still. To capture more light, your iPhone is reducing the shutter speed. However, blurring action is achieved with a slower shutter speed.

If you want a clear, blur-free photo while shooting in Night mode, hold your phone steady. Use a steady surface to prop up the phone, or invest in a tripod. When using only your hands, keep the gadget stable by drawing your elbows close to your torso.

Because the camera has electronic and optical picture stabilization, it can handle slight motions quite well.

2. Set The Timer On Your Camera

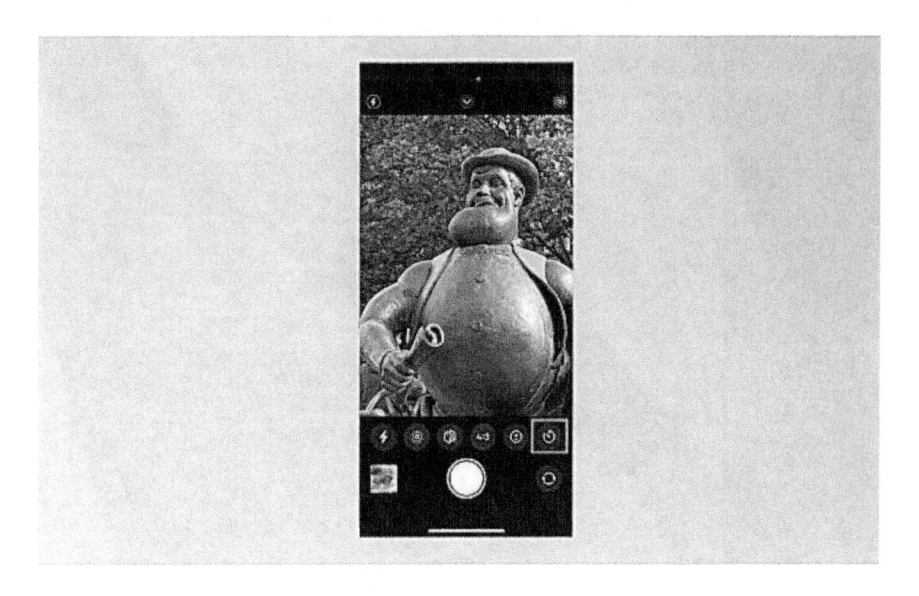

Obviously, not holding the phone steady is the best approach to taking a steady photo. So, the camera won't be shaken by your hand or body movements. Using a tripod or just setting the phone on a surface are also viable options, as we indicated before.

For instance, how do you ensure that you are included in a group photo? Use the self-timer! It's that easy! If you're confused about how to utilize the self-timer feature on your iPhone, we've got you covered with a useful tutorial.

3. Pick Your Fields Of Study

Recall how blurry moving objects seem with slow shutter speeds. That's just as true for your unsteady hands as it is for the people in your photographs. Shutter rates that are too slow cause blurring of any moving subjects in the photo.

That being said, low light isn't ideal for subjects like a bouncing kid or a jogging dog. If possible, try to shoot stationary objects while working with low light. Try to get your subjects to be as still as possible if you really must snap pictures of them.

4. Limit The Amount Of Radiation

Even in Night mode, the exposure slider allows you to tweak the brightness of your images if they seem too bright. By tapping and swiping up or down on the viewfinder, you may adjust the exposure.

Another alternative is to access the camera's settings by tapping the arrow that appears above the viewfinder. From there, choose Exposure (the symbol with the plus and minus signs), and adjust the exposure slider as needed.

5. **When It's Not Needed, Disable Night Mode.**

Overexposure may occur if night mode is used unintentionally. Because of this, regular images may seem too bright, and the highlights may even be blown out.

Just turn on Night mode when you need it. To remove Night mode from your camera app, tap the moon symbol located in the upper left corner.

HOW TO TAKE APPLE PRORAW PHOTOS WITH YOUR IPHONE CAMERA

You may capture photographs in Apple ProRAW using the Camera on compatible devices. By fusing the data from a conventional RAW format with the picture processing capabilities of an iPhone, Apple ProRAW gives you more leeway to express your creativity when adjusting white balance, exposure, and color.

The front-facing camera, like all the others, supports Apple ProRAW. Using Portrait mode with Apple ProRAW is not supported.

SET UP APPLE PRORAW

Navigate to Settings > Camera > Formats on devices that support it to activate Apple ProRAW or ProRAW & Resolution Control.

Keep in mind that the larger file sizes are because Apple ProRAW images retain more information.

Once you've taken a photo using the Apple ProRAW Open Camera, just press the Raw Off button (or the Raw 12 Switch Button Off button, depending on your model) to activate ProRAW.

TAKE A PHOTO WITH APPLE PRORAW

1. As you shoot, you can toggle ProRAW on and off by pressing the Raw On button, the Raw Off button, or the Raw 12 Switch Button On and Off buttons.
2. To save your ProRAW settings, activate either Apple ProRAW or ProRAW & Resolution

Control (whatever applies to your model) in the Settings menu, then go to the Camera section and choose Preserve Settings.

MODIFY THE PRE-SET FORMAT AND RESOLUTION OF APPLE PRORAW.

Depending on your model, you may choose between 12 MP, 48 MP, or HEIF 48 MP as the default ProRAW resolution for the iPhone 15 Pro, iPhone 15 Pro Max, 14, Pro, and 14 Pro.

1. Find Formats in the Settings menu, then go to Camera.
2. Adjust the resolution and enable ProRAW.
3. Select ProRAW 12 MP, ProRAW Max, or HEIF Max from the list of available resolutions and formats by tapping the Pro Default button.

Note: JPEG Max will be used instead of HEIF Max if you have selected Most Compatible as your Camera Capture preset.

CHAPTER SEVEN

HOW TO RECORD VIDEOS WITH YOUR IPHONE CAMERA

To capture video and QuickTime movies on your iPhone, use the Camera app. Discover the ins and outs of switching between cinematic, slow-motion, and time-lapse modes.

Note: Video recording cannot be done while on a phone or FaceTime call.

RECORD A VIDEO

1. To change the camera's video mode, open the camera app and follow the on-screen instructions.
2. To begin recording, either press the volume buttons or tap the Record button. Here are some things you can do while recording:
    - The white Shutter button may be used to capture a static image.
    - You may zoom in and out by pinching the screen.
    - On devices that enable it, you can get a finer zoom by touching and holding the 1x button and dragging the slider.

3. To end the recording, either tap the Record button or push the volume buttons simultaneously.

Note: A green dot will display at the top of the screen whenever the Camera is in use for your security.

TAKE HIGH-DEFINITION OR ULTRA-HIGH-DEFINITION FOOTAGE.

You may capture video in many high-quality formats on your iPhone, including HD, 4K, HD (PAL), and 4K (PAL).

1. To record a video, open the camera app and go to the settings menu.
2. Choose an option from the supported video formats and frame rates for your iPhone.

Note: Video files will be bigger with faster frame rates and better resolutions. Many nations and areas in South America, Asia, Africa, and Europe use the PAL television visual format.

TURN ON ACTION MODE.

When capturing video on an iPhone 14 or 15 using the "Action" setting, the device is more stable. You may toggle Action mode on and off by tapping the corresponding buttons on the screen.

Note: In strong light, action mode performs at its finest. Go to the Settings menu, then touch Camera. From there, choose Record Video. Finally, enable Action Mode Lower Light if you want to utilize Action Mode in low light. The highest resolution that can be captured in action mode is 2.8K.

CAPTURE A VIDEO WITH QUICKTAKE

If you record a video in Photo mode, it will be a QuickTake video. Locking the Record button allows you to continue snapping still photographs even as you record a QuickTake movie.

1. To begin shooting a QuickTake video, open the Camera app and press and hold the Shutter button.
2. To record without using your hands, slide the shutter button to the right and release it when you see the lock.

- Below the frame, you'll see the Record and Shutter buttons. To capture a still shot while recording, just hit the Shutter button.
- If you're filming without using your hands, you can pinch out on the screen to zoom in, or you may swipe up to focus on your subject.

3. You may stop recording by tapping the Record button.

Tip: To begin recording a QuickTake video in Photo mode, press and hold the volume up or down button.

To see the QuickTake movie on the Photos app, tap on the thumbnail.

CAPTURE A VIDEO IN SLOW MOTION.

The video records normally in slow-motion mode, but when you play it back, it seems like it was shot in slow motion. You may also set a start and end time for the slow-motion effect in your video editing software.

1. Go to the camera and choose the slow-motion option.

    To record in slow-motion mode using the front camera on iPhone 11, 12, 13, 14, and 15 models, press the Camera Chooser Back-Facing button.

2. To begin recording, either press the volume buttons or tap the Record button.

    To capture a still image while recording, just press the Shutter button.

3. To end the recording, either tap the Record button or push the volume buttons simultaneously.

Press the video thumbnail, then choose Edit to have part of the video play at a slower pace while the remaining part plays normally. To set the frame viewer to play in slow motion, drag the vertical bars underneath it.

Slow motion's frame rate and resolution are model-specific. Press Record Slo-mo after going to Settings > Camera to adjust the slow-motion recording options.

Hint: You can change the video's resolution and frame rate with the press of a button during recording. Refer to Toggle between different video resolutions and frame rates with ease.

Create A Time-Lapse Film.

To make a time-lapse film of an event that happens over some time, such as the sun setting or traffic moving, record footage at certain intervals.

1. To switch to time-lapse mode, open the camera app.
2. Prepare your iPhone to record a moving scene.
3. If you want to start or stop recording, just hit the Record button.

Advice: If you're shooting time-lapse films in low light with an iPhone 12 or later, a tripod will help you get more clarity and light.

HOW TO TAKE A SCREEN RECORDING ON IPHONE

Using your iPhone, you can capture the screen's activity.

- Find Screen Recording in the Settings menu, then press the Control Center button. From there, hit the Insert Screen Recording button.
- After you've opened Control Center and tapped the Screen Recording button, just wait for the 3-second countdown to finish.
- To end recording, launch Control Center, press the red status bar or the Selected Screen Recording button, and finally, hit Stop.

When you record your screen, the Photos app will add the clip to your library. Open Photos, then touch Albums. Then, hit Screen Recordings, which is located underneath Media Types, to see all of your screen recordings in one convenient location.

HOW TO USE THE APPLE PRORES ON THE IPHONE

RECORD VIDEO IN APPLE PRORES

The Camera app's Video mode allows you to capture footage in Apple ProRes format with any of its cameras.

If your video editing program supports Apple ProRes, you may edit it with iMovie or Photos on Mac, Final Cut Pro on iPad and Mac, or any other app that supports Apple ProRes. Get the lowdown on Apple's ProRes and ProRes RAW formats.

Cinematic mode, slow motion, and time-lapse footage are not compatible with ProRes.

WHAT YOU NEED

One of the following iPhone models is required to utilize Apple ProRes, along with iOS 15.1 or later:

- iPhone 15 Pro Max
- iPhone 15 Pro
- iPhone 14 Pro Max
- iPhone 14 Pro
- iPhone 13 Pro Max
- iPhone 13 Pro

Find Out What Screen Sizes And Frame Rates Are Compatible.

High dynamic range (HDR), standard dynamic range (SDR), and log encoding are all ProRes recording options that are compatible with your iPhone while utilizing its internal storage.

If you have an external storage device that is connected via USB-C, you can record in Apple ProRes format with the iPhone 15 Pro and iPhone 15 Pro Max.

Here are several resolutions and frame speeds that your iPhone can handle:

- Fully compatible with ProRes for storage capacities of 256 GB, 512 GB, and 1 TB:
  - Only the iPhone 15 Pro and iPhone 15 Pro Max, with an external storage device that can handle rates of at least 220 MB per second and a maximum power demand of 4.5W, can achieve 4K at 60 frames per second.
  - Stunning 4K at 30, 25, and 24 frames per second is available.
  - Full HD at 60, 30, and 25 frames per second
- Up to 128 GB of storage space is supported by ProRes:
  - 30 and 25 frames per second in 1080p HD
  - Only the iPhone 15 Pro and iPhone 15 Pro Max, with an external storage device that can handle rates of at least 220 MB per second and a maximum power demand of 4.5W, can achieve 4K at 60 frames per second.

Enable ProRes

Go to the iPhone's Settings > Camera > Formats, and then enable Apple ProRes under Video Capture to record videos in ProRes. You can record a video in ProRes format by going to the Camera app and tapping the ProRes Apple.

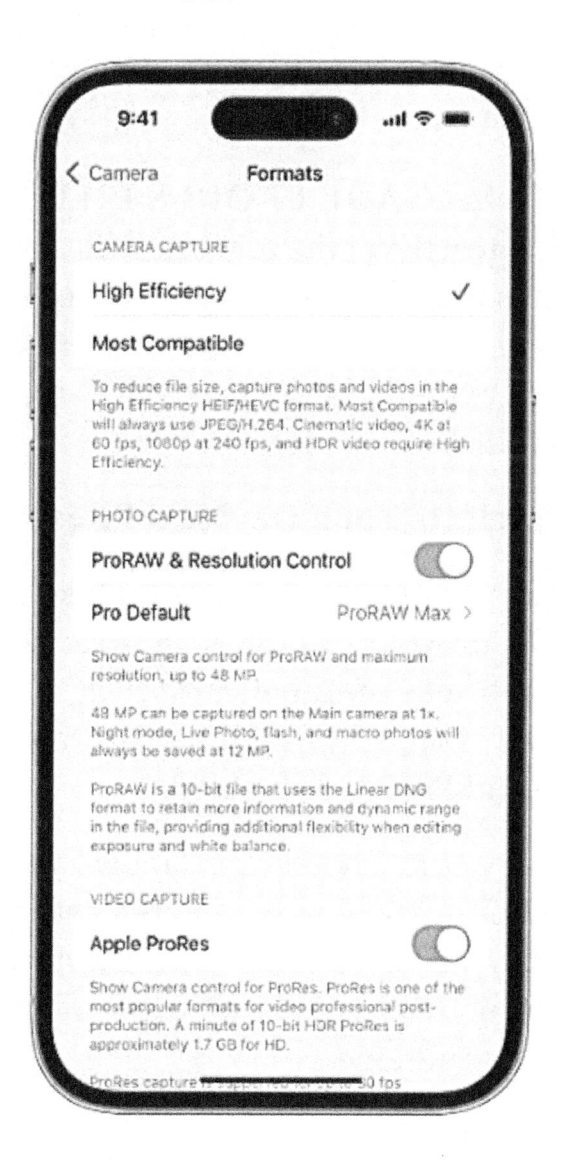

You may choose between High-Efficiency Video Coding (HEVC) and Most Compatible (H.264) as the default video format in Camera Capture, which is accessible via Settings > Camera > Formats when you disable ProRes in the Camera app.

MANAGE PRORES FILES

Compared to HEVC files, ProRes files might be up to 30 times bigger. If you own an iPhone, iCloud, or an iPhone 15 Pro or iPhone 15 Pro Max, you may use a USB-C external storage device to store and manage your ProRes files.

Keep Track Of Your Device's Files

If you want to record in ProRes, make sure that at least 10% of your iPhone's storage is free. The Camera app may automatically clear storage if you have fewer than five minutes of recording time available and ProRes is enabled.

Additionally, the Photos app allows you to export big films or images to a separate storage device. Next, remove the video from the Photos app and finally from the Recently Deleted album to make room on your iPhone.

Control Your iCloud Files

If you want to keep your images in iCloud images, you may have to increase your iCloud storage plan so that there's more room for these bigger files. Also, file size limitations are using iCloud.

Save ProRes Files To A Portable Hard Drive

If you own an iPhone 15 Pro or 15 Pro Max, you may record or save your ProRes files straight on an external storage device thanks to the USB-C connector. Several considerations are outlined below:

- The APFS or exFAT file system is required for your external storage device. We don't support disks that are encrypted with passwords.
- Connect with a USB 3.0 connection that can handle data transfers of 10 Gbit/s or faster.
- A minimum of 220 MB/s of writing speed is required of your external storage device. A Slow Recording Speed notice may appear if you connect an external storage device that isn't very fast.
- To manage your ProRes files and format your external storage drive, use the Files app.
- Disconnect the external storage device before you may record to your iPhone.

USE THE PRORES WITH PHOTOS AND OTHER APPS

Apps that are compatible with the Apple ProRes format may open ProRes files because of the format's broad use in the video post-production industry. If an app doesn't support ProRes, it may convert the video to the lower H.264 format.

Change A ProRes File

Photos and iMovie on iOS devices, Final Cut Pro on Mac and iPad, and other editing tools that handle Apple ProRes files are all compatible with editing these files.

You can play back and edit in ProRes on these Apple devices:

- Mac with Mac OS X 10.6 and later
- iPad Pro 12.9-inch (3rd generation) and later
- iPad Pro 11-inch (1st generation) and later
- iPad Air (5th generation)
- iPad mini (6th generation)
- iPhone 15, iPhone 15 Plus, iPhone 15 Pro, iPhone 15 Pro Max
- iPhone 14, iPhone 14 Plus, iPhone 14 Pro, iPhone 14 Pro Max
- iPhone 13 mini, iPhone 13, iPhone 13 Pro, iPhone 13 Pro Max

SHARE PRORES VIDEO

Sending a ProRes video:

- To transmit the files, you'll need a USB-C or Lightning connector along with Image Capture for Mac or a similar tool for Windows PC.
- Put your ProRes video file on an external drive.
- All of your devices may see the original, high-resolution ProRes video file thanks to iCloud Photos.
- Import the ProRes file into Final Cut Pro on your Mac, iPad, or another iOS device via AirDrop. After you've enabled All Photos Data by tapping the Options button at the top of the page, hit Done. When you use AirDrop, your original ProRes video can be transferred to the following devices: certain models of the iPhone (15, 14, and 13), Macs running Mac OS X 10.6 or later, iPads (12.9-inch and 11-inch Pro models), iPad Air (5th generation), and iPad mini (6th generation). If the device supports HEVC, you'll share an HEVC video; otherwise, you'll send an H.264 video.

HOW TO USE CINEMATIC MODE ON YOUR IPHONE

A cinematic effect may be achieved with your iPhone camera by switching to Cinematic mode. This allows you to capture films with a narrow depth of field and create stunning focus transitions.

Please ensure that you are using an iPhone capable of filming in Cinematic mode and that you are running the most recent version of iOS before proceeding:

- iPhone 15 Pro Max
- iPhone 15 Pro
- iPhone 15
- iPhone 15 Plus
- iPhone 14 Pro Max
- iPhone 14 Pro
- iPhone 14

- iPhone 14 Plus
- iPhone 13 Pro Max
- iPhone 13 Pro
- iPhone 13
- iPhone 13 mini

HOW TO RECORD VIDEO IN CINEMATIC MODE

- Pull up the Camera app and tap the Cinematic mode button.
- To access these customization options in landscape mode, tap the arrow:

- To modify the depth of field, use the Depth Control button and move the slider.
- To get to Telephoto mode, press the 1x button. Pressing the button again (it will now say 3x) will return it to Wide.

- Press the exposure button and adjust the brightness or darkness of your video by dragging the slider.
- Select Auto, On, or Off by tapping the flash button.
* To start recording, press the record button.
* As you record, tap the viewfinder to concentrate on a different topic. To enable subject-based automatic focus tracking, double-tap. To fix the focus at a certain distance from the camera, you may also press and hold the screen.
* Repeat the process of tapping the record button to end the recording.

Dolby Vision HDR is compatible with cinematic mode. You may choose between 24/25 or 30 frames per second in Cinematic mode on the iPhone 14.

EDIT VIDEO TAKEN IN CINEMATIC MODE

Your iPhone 14 or another compatible device's Photos app will allow you to edit videos shot in Cinematic mode.

You can edit any film with the usual tools, but in Cinematic mode, you can also change the focus points and depth of field.

You will need iOS 16, iPadOS 16, or macOS Ventura or later to edit films captured on iOS 16 in Cinematic mode.

How To Edit Depth Of Field In A Video Taken In Cinematic Mode

- Launch the Photos app and choose the video you want to edit.
- Select Edit.
- To modify the depth of field, use the Depth Control button and move the slider. Every frame of the movie will be affected by your depth of field adjustments.

- Press Finish.

How To Edit Focus Points In A Video Taken In Cinematic Mode

- Launch the Photos app and choose the video you want to edit.
- Select Edit. What you see underneath your video is the video timeline. Additionally, the yellow dots underneath the timeline indicate points in the movie when the camera pans to a different topic.
- To navigate through your movie, just drag the timeline indication button. A yellow square will appear to show you where the video is currently focused as you drag it. A white square encircles other identified individuals or things.
- By tapping on a white square, you may shift the camera's focus to that specific subject. To switch the emphasis to another item in the frame, you may also touch on it. To enable automatic focus tracking, double-tap a topic. To fix the focus at a certain distance from the camera, tap and hold the screen.

- To toggle between the Camera app's built-in focus tracking and the spots you've manually chosen, just tap the focus button.
- After you've done so for all the parts of the video that you want to refocus, hit the Done button.

Hold down the yellow dot until the delete button shows, then press it, to remove a focus point transition.

Transfer Cinematic Effects To Other Devices For Editing

Any of the following devices running iOS 15 or later may have the Photos app enhanced with Cinematic mode video effects:

- iPhone XS, iPhone XR, and later
- iPad Pro 12.9-inch (3rd generation and later)

- iPad Pro 11-inch (1st generation and later)
- iPad Air (3rd generation and later)
- iPad mini (5th generation and later)

Use iCloud Photos or AirDrop to ensure that a movie shot in Cinematic mode may be edited on another compatible device. Make sure to enable All Photos Data before sending using AirDrop:

- To share a video, use the Photos app and then touch on the video.
- After tapping the Share icon, go to the top of the screen and select Options.
- To enable all photo data, hit the "Done" button.
- Select the recipient's device by tapping the AirDrop button.

HOW TO ADJUST HDR SETTINGS ON IPHONE

With Camera's HDR (high dynamic range) feature, you can capture stunning images even in very dark or bright environments. The iPhone quickly snaps many images with varying exposures and then combines them to enhance the detail in your photos, both in the highlights and the shadows.

When it's optimal, the iPhone automatically captures images in high dynamic range (HDR) using both the back and front cameras. Video recorded with an iPhone 12, 13, 14, or 15 uses high dynamic range (HDR) to capture colors and contrasts as they appear.

Disable HDR Auto-Focus.

When it's most effective, the iPhone automatically employs HDR. As an alternative, you may manually adjust HDR on certain iPhone models.

Turn off Smart HDR in the Camera app's settings on iPhone XS, XR, 11 models, SE (2nd gen), and 12 models. Next, toggle HDR on or off from the camera's interface.

Initiate And Deactivate HDR Video.

Dolby Vision HDR allows for more accurate color and contrast while recording video on iPhone 12, 13, 14, and 15 models. Navigate to Settings > Camera > Record Video to disable high dynamic range video recording.

CHAPTER EIGHT

HOW TO TURN OFF THE CAMERA SOUND ON IPHONE

On iPhone 15 Models, Use The Mute Button Or Ring/Silent Switch

Haptic is the new Camera Sound on the iPhone 15 Pro (Max) series. Customers will not be able to hear the shutter release while taking pictures using the Camera app.

Keep pressing the action button until you hear a beep to toggle between silence and ring, or ring and silent. The dynamic island displays the outcome. or Turn off Silent Mode by disabling the toggle in the Sounds & Haptics section of the Settings menu. or Press the bell symbol in the control center to activate quiet mode.

1. Locate the mute button on the upper left side of your iPhone.
2. Gently slide the mute button from bottom to top. Additionally, while your iPhone is in muted mode, a little orange dot will appear above the button.

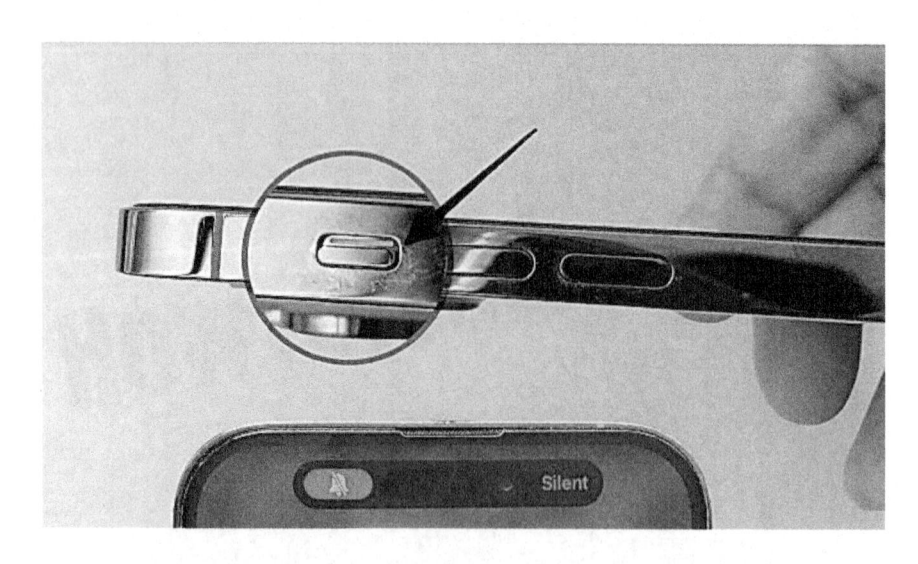

3. Get the shutter sound to go away by taking a picture using your iPhone's real camera.

Will Muting The Camera Sound Also Silence The iPhone?

A lot of people want to disable the quiet mode without really turning off the camera's shutter sound. Regrettably, there is currently no set method for doing it. For instance, most people who use Snapchat are probably trying to figure out how to silence the camera on an iPhone without muting the app itself. Consequently, there is no option for this particular app configuration either. If you are looking for an app that provides this, you can find them on the app store.

USING ASSISTIVE TOUCH WITHOUT THE RINGER OR SILENT RELAY

In the iPhone's settings, locate the Accessibility app, tap Hit Touch, then tap Assistive Touch. Finally, turn the toggle next to the AssitiveTouch on or green to enable assistive touch and customization.

1. Open the Settings app on your iPhone. Then, tap on Accessibility.

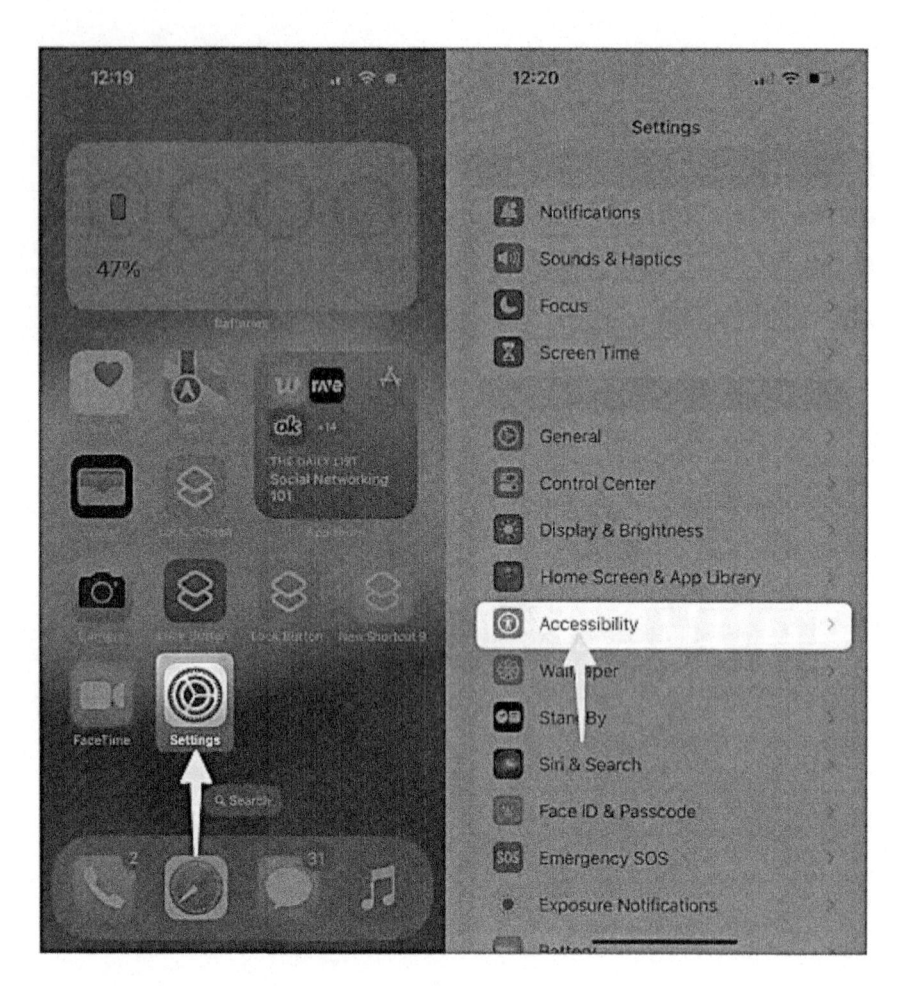

2. Choose Touch.
3. Enable the AssistiveTouch toggle by tapping on it.

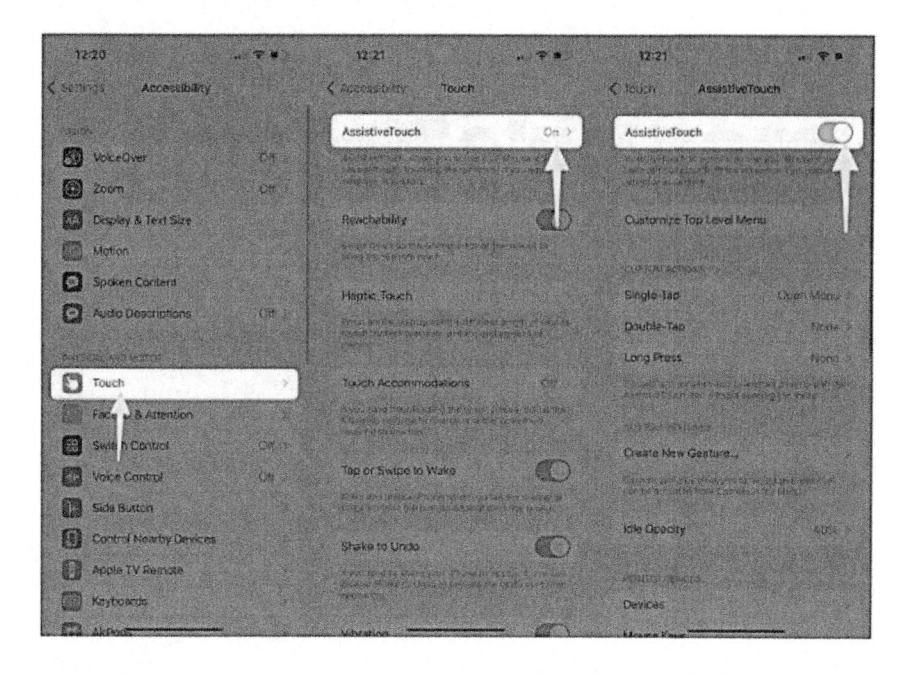

4. Press the touch button, which is also called the assistive touch button.
5. Disable the camera's shutter sound by tapping the Device icon and then selecting mute.

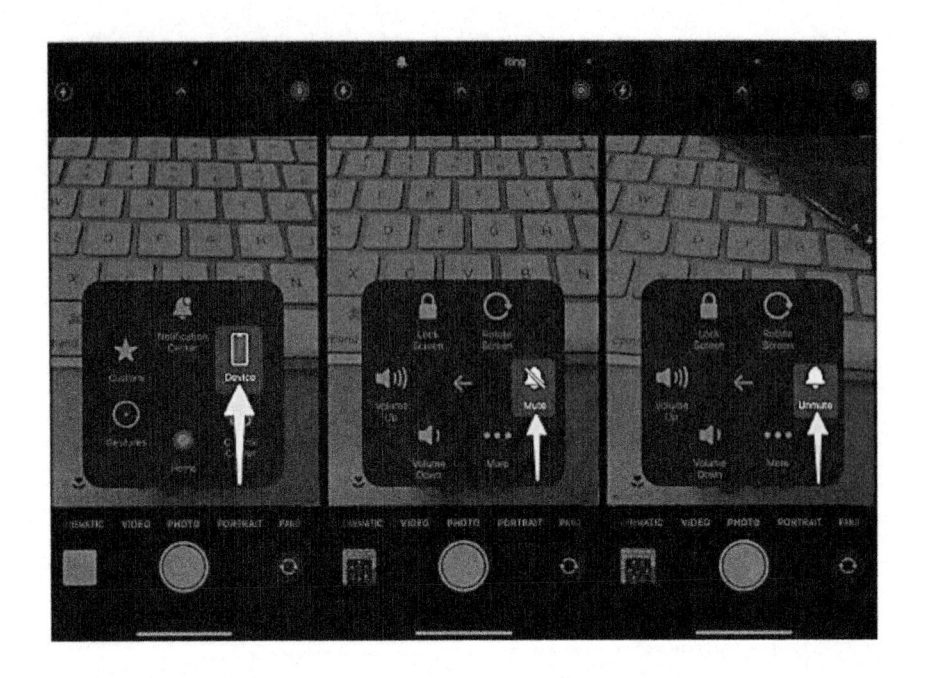

Right now If you want to avoid hearing the shutter release when you open the camera app, As we snap the photo using the iOS camera app, the user presses the shutter button.

Below, you can see the interface where you may turn on the camera's sound and turn it off.

DECREASE CAMERA CLICK VOLUME: MUTE THE CLICK-CLICK-CLICK

Use the iPhone's volume down button to adjust the volume before opening the camera app.

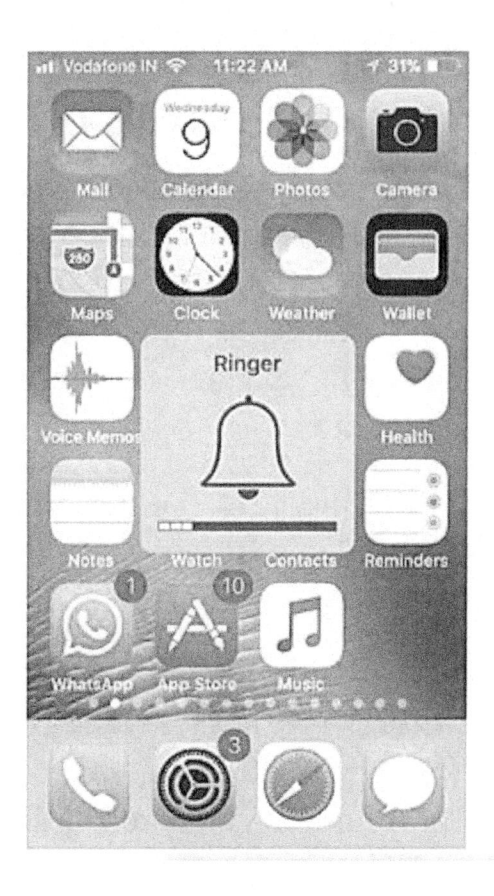

Additionally, make sure you're clicking the camera correctly. To record audio, just press the camera's capture button.

Note: Those who are unable to use the Physical button (Ring/Silent Button) may find this approach useful. This button has been damaged.

HOW TO CHANGE THE CAMERA'S VIDEO RECORDING SETTINGS ON IPHONE

The camera typically captures video at a frame rate of 30 fps. Various options for video resolution and frame rate are available on different iPhone models. Video files become bigger as frame rates and resolutions go greater.

The camera interface also has fast toggles that let you modify the video's frame rate and quality with ease.

ALTER THE VIDEO'S FRAME RATE AND RESOLUTION WITH THE PUSH OF A BUTTON.

To adjust the iPhone's video resolution and frame rate when in Video mode, utilize the quick toggles located at the screen's top.

Depending on your model, you may quickly shift between 4K and HD recording, as well as 24, 25, 30, or 60 fps in Video mode, by tapping the fast toggles in the top-right corner.

In Cinematic mode, you may quickly transition between high definition (HD) and ultra-high definition (4K) at 24, 25, or 30 frames per second on iPhone 14 and iPhone 15 models.

ADJUST THE AUTO FPS SETTINGS

Automatically lowering the frame rate to 24 fps, the iPhone may enhance video quality in low-light conditions.

Depending on your model, perform one of the following after going to Settings > Camera > Record Video:

- Select Auto FPS from the menu. You may then choose to use it on 30-frame videos exclusively or on both 30- and 60-frame videos.
- Saddle up the Auto Low Light FPS.

TURN STEREO RECORDING ON AND OFF

Stereo sound is achieved by the use of numerous microphones on the iPhone.

Navigate to the Settings menu, then choose Camera. From there, disable the option to Record Stereo Sound.

ACTIVATE AND DEACTIVATE HIGH DYNAMIC RANGE (HDR) VIDEO.

Using iOS 13.4, iPadOS 13.4, macOS 10.15.4, or later, the iPhone may capture video in high dynamic range (HDR) and share these recordings with other devices; devices without these systems will get a standard dynamic range (SDR) version of the same video.

You may disable high dynamic range recording by going to the following menu: Settings > Camera > Record Video.

ALTER THE STATE OF THE LOCK CAMERA.
The Lock Camera feature stops the iPhone 13, 14, and 15 from automatically switching cameras when recording video. By default, the Lock Camera is turned off.

To enable Lock Camera, go to Settings > Camera > Record Video, and finally, toggle the switch to the on position.

TOGGLE THE SWITCH FOR ENHANCED STABILIZATION.
When using Video or Cinematic mode to record, the Enhanced stability feature on iPhone 14 and iPhone 15 models significantly magnifies the image for better stability. Automatically enabled is Enhanced Stabilization.

You may disable Enhanced Stabilization by going to Settings > Camera > Record Video.

DEACTIVATE AND ACTIVATE THE LOCK WHITE BALANCE.

When shooting movies on an iPhone, you have the option to lock the white balance. This will allow for more precise color capture regardless of the lighting circumstances.

Navigate to the Settings menu, then choose Camera. From there, choose Record Video. Finally, toggle the Lock White Balance switch on.

CHAPTER NINE

WHAT IS LIVE TEXT ON IPHONE

With a plethora of brand-new capabilities, Live Text is a remarkable new tool. It lets you scan and copy text inside photographs, much like your iPhone's built-in optical character recognition capability. It can copy text or numbers and then you may utilize them for a variety of purposes, such as sending emails, translating text, and making calls.

With Live Text, you can instantly add text to photos taken with the Camera, Photos, or Safari applications. Pressing the indication icon will begin the process.

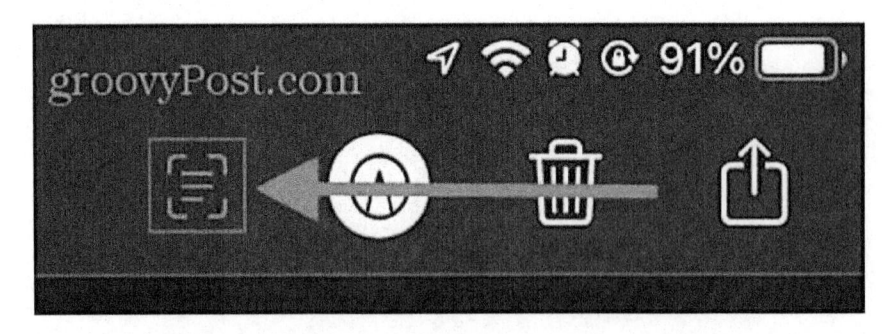

HOW TO ACTIVATE LIVE TEXT

It is not necessary to toggle Live Text on or off. To utilize it with other languages, however, you must enable it.

On an iPhone, to enable Live Text:

- On your iPhone, open the Settings app.
- Click on General.
- Choose your language and choose your region.
- To enable Live Text, just toggle its slider.

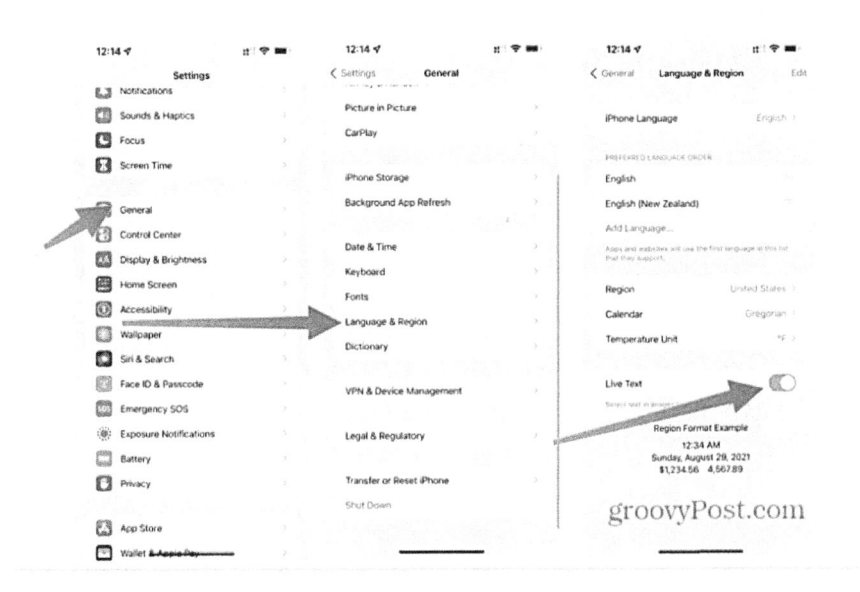

Using Live Text On iPhone

The Live Text tool has several helpful features that you may make use of. Copying text, making calls, sending emails, searching online or in a local dictionary, and many other features are all part of it.

Using Live Text is as simple as following these instructions.

How To Copy Text Within An Image

In either Safari or Photos, you'll discover a Live Text option that allows you to copy text from images. Afterward, you'll be free to recycle the text.

To use Live Text to copy text from an image:

- Pick out the picture.
- Toggle the indication button.
- Hold down the image's visible text or number with your finger.
- To choose a whole word or number, just drag the selector. Choose All as an alternative.
- To copy it to the clipboard, use the Copy button.

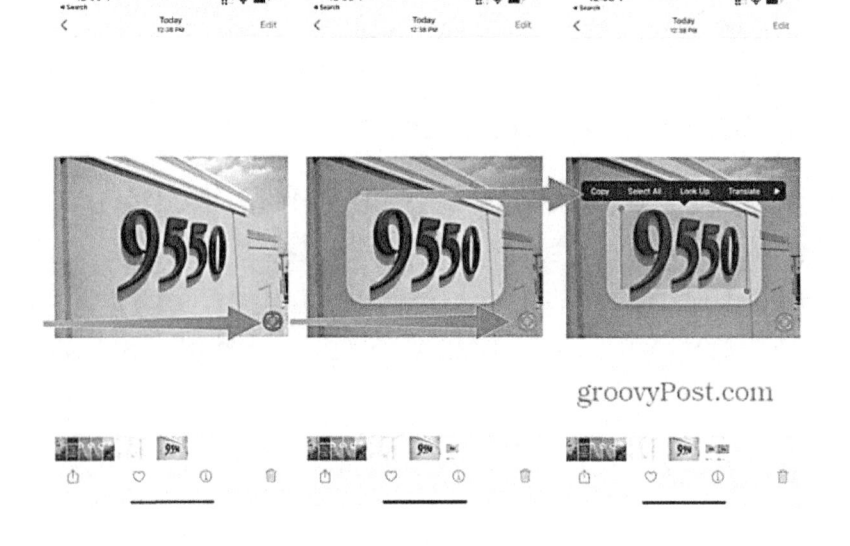

Methods For Dialing A Number Or Writing An Email

You may make a call or send an email by clicking on the phone number or email address that appears in an image or picture.

Using Live Text to send an email or make a phone call:

- Find the photo with the caption and choose it using the Photos software on your computer.
- Locate and choose the symbol representing the indication.
- Select the email or phone number.
- Select Call to make a phone call, and select Send Message to send an email. Additional options to make a FaceTime call or add to contacts may appear depending on the URL.

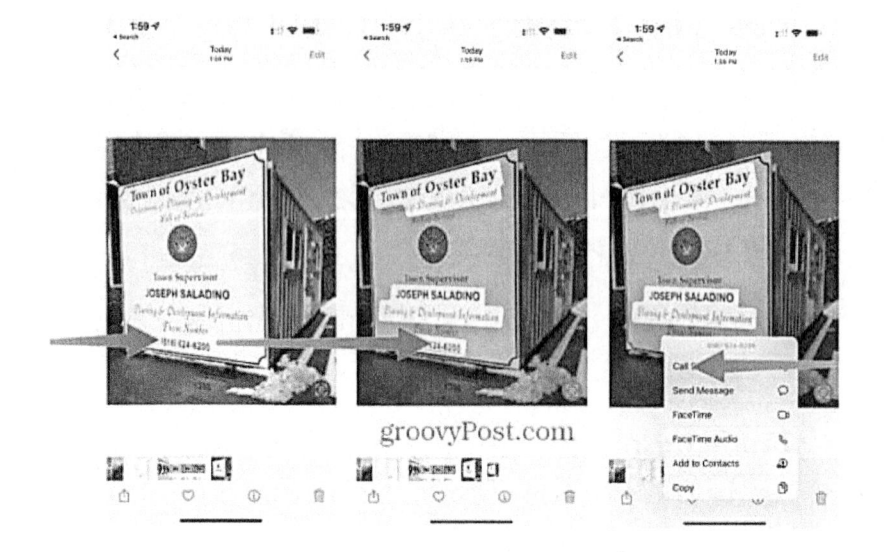

How To Translate Text Using Live Text

Live Text's translation tool supports a wide range of languages, allowing you to convert text into pictures into many more. Among them are languages spoken throughout the world, from Chinese to French and Italian in Europe.

For Live Text to translate text:

- Find the photo with the caption and choose it using the Photos software on your computer.
- Locate and choose the symbol representing the indication.
- To change your selection, touch and hold the word. Then, drag the grab points as needed.
- Click on Translate.

- Select the target language for the translation by tapping Continue, if prompted. Or you may choose to switch languages.

Caution: Before translating, you may need to download the language(s) in question. To accomplish this, follow any extra instructions that may appear on the screen.

HOW TO SEARCH A DICTIONARY OR ONLINE

Live Text is another tool you may use to learn more about a subject. You may utilize a picture as a search engine if it has words related to a topic. Your iPhone will instead look it up in the local dictionary if it's only a single word.

To do an internet search using Live Text:

- Launch the Photos app and choose the picture that has the words you want to look up online.
- To access the indication, tap the symbol in the app.
- Using the two grab points on each side of the picture, pick out the whole phrase or number.
- You may look it up online by tapping the Look Up option.

With Look Up, you may access a dictionary by selecting a single word. When that isn't the case, a list of related websites and videos will appear.

How To Use Visual Look-Up With Live Text

One more thing: the Visual Look Up feature may tell you more about things in a picture. Things in your shot that fall under this category may be anything from landmarks to flora to pets.

To access Live Text's Visual Look-Up functions:

- Launch Photos to access your picture.
- Press and hold the Visual Up icon.
- Find the symbol either within or below the picture and click on it. Animals and pets have

paw symbols, whereas plants and flowers have a leaf image.

In the absence of a Visual Look Up button, any picture or photograph cannot be identified.

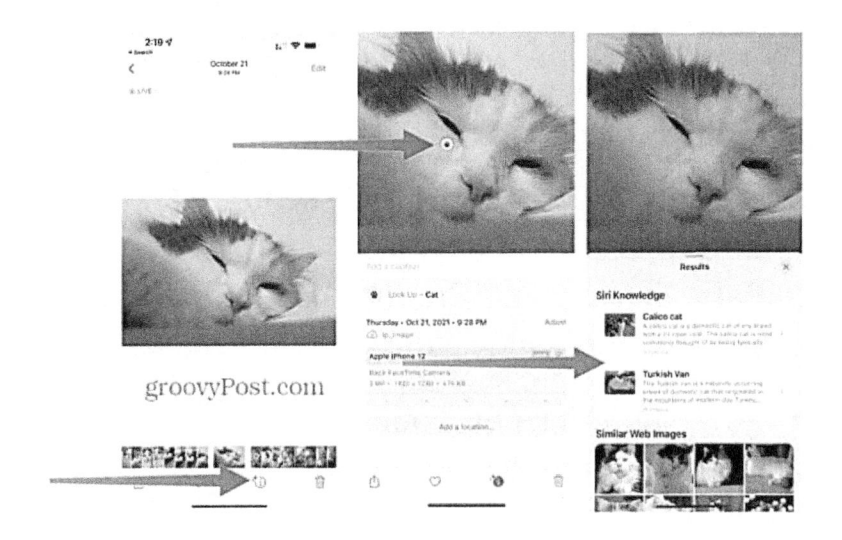

Expanding The Use Of Live Text To Other Media

Although Live Text is exclusive to iOS devices, it is also compatible with Macs running Monterey and later.

You may use the characters in a picture to copy and paste or even make a phone call with Live Text. Another feature that allows you to learn more about a location, structure, or item is an integrated translation tool. Visual Look Up expands your knowledge of many things, including animals, locations, and more.

HOW TO VIEW PHOTOS AND VIDEOS SHARED WITH YOU ON IPHONE

Stream media from friends' iPhones to yours

You can quickly locate the media files that someone has shared with you in the Messages app under the Photos app's Shared with You section. (Make sure your buddy is in your contacts and that you have Automatic Sharing and Photos enabled in Settings > Messages > Shared with You.)

1. After tapping For You, find Shared with You and scroll down.
2. Perform one of these tasks:
    - If you want to see a picture in full screen, download it, share it, or remove it, just tap on it.
    - To see all of the shared photographs, use the See All button.
    - To respond to the photo's sharer, open the Messages app and tap on their name.

To see media files sent to you via Messages, you may alternatively go to the Library and choose All Photos. A conversation bubble may be seen in the bottom-left corner of the thumbnail for these photographs and videos. To share, save, or delete an image or video, just tap on its thumbnail. Select Your Photos Only from the More Options menu to conceal media files sent to you via Messages.

Note: If you delete a conversation in Messages, all of the media files in Shared with You and your library will be deleted as well.

Then go to Messages in Settings, followed by Shared with You. Select Photos from the menu, and then turn it off (green means on).

CHAPTER TEN

HOW TO MAKE A FACETIME CALL ON IPHONE

The use of video calls has been on the increase in recent years, and it's easy to understand why: they allow us to stay in touch even when we can't be physically there. If you possess an iPhone, iPad, or Mac, you probably already have Apple's video calling program, FaceTime, installed on your device. Seeing and interacting with your favorite individuals is as easy as tapping a few buttons, provided you have Wi-Fi or a cellular data connection.

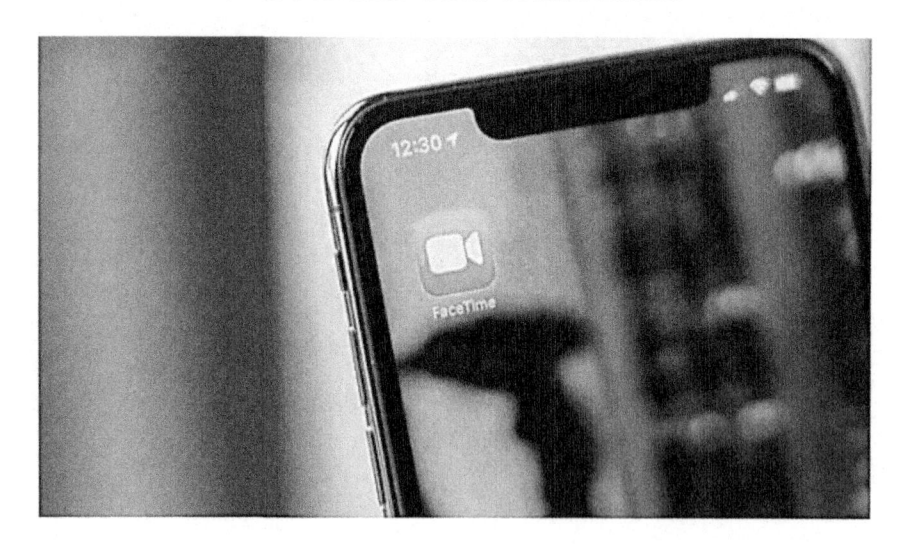

HOW TO MAKE A NEW FACETIME CALL
1. Start up FaceTime on your iOS device.

2. Click on the "New FaceTime" icon.

3. Indicate which people you would want to initiate a FaceTime call with. A phone number, email address, or name will suffice for this purpose.
4. Just keep adding names, email addresses, or phone numbers until you have everyone in your group for FaceTime.
5. Press the button to initiate a FaceTime call, either audio or video.

HOW TO TURN OFF VIDEO OR MUTE YOURSELF WHILE ON A FACETIME CALL

1. You may initiate or join a FaceTime call.
2. On the call, you may access the floating toolbar by tapping the microphone or camera toggle.

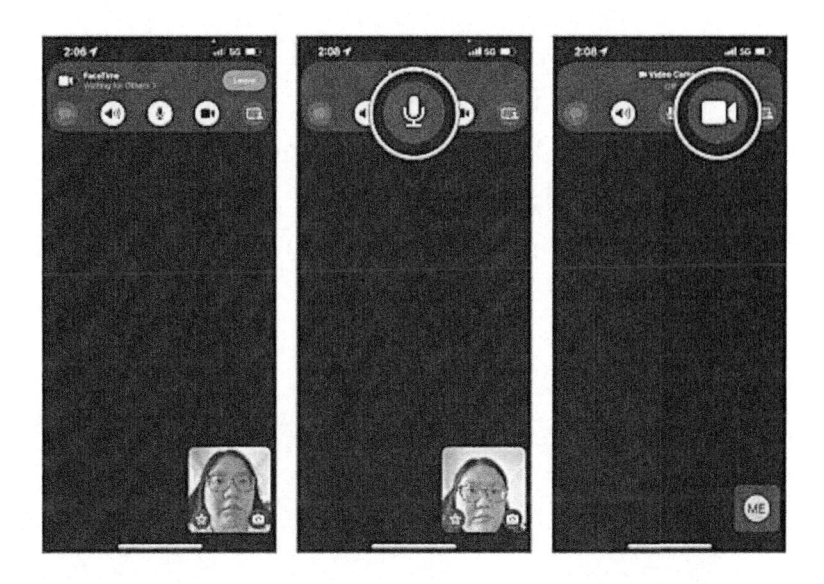

If you're using FaceTime while muted, you'll get a message that says so; tapping the notification will unmute you. This functionality is included in iOS and iPadOS.

MAKING A FACETIME CALL LINK ON DEVICES OTHER THAN APPLE

Apple also offers the option to let devices that aren't Apple products join FaceTime conversations. The catch is that you have to make a FaceTime conversation connection before you can accomplish this.

Whether you're using an iPhone, iPad, or Mac, you can set up a FaceTime call connection.

HOW TO MAKE A FACETIME AUDIO OR VIDEO CALL ON IOS 14 AND OLDER

1. Use your iOS device to launch FaceTime.
2. Click the plus sign.
3. Simply enter the desired contact's name, email address, or phone number.
4. To make a group call, just type in additional names, emails, or phone numbers.
5. Press the Audio or Video button to initiate the call.

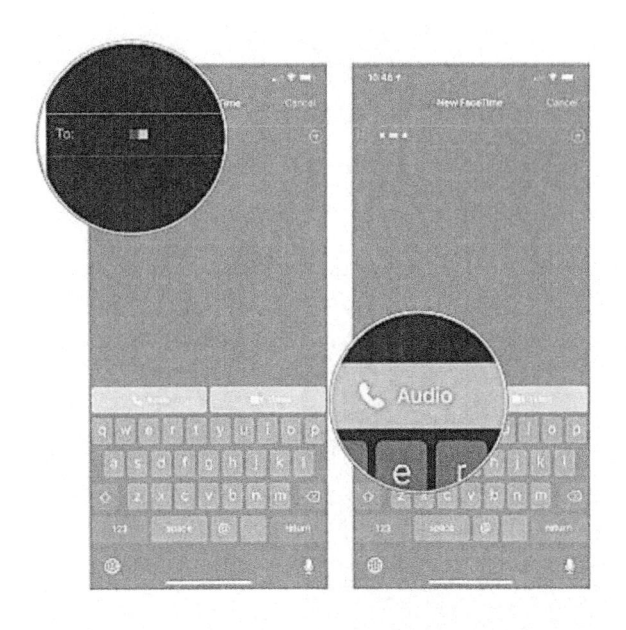

HOW TO SWITCH FROM A REGULAR CALL TO FACETIME ON YOUR IPHONE

1. While on the phone, you should examine the call menu.
2. To start a FaceTime video call, just tap the button.

HOW TO TURN OFF VIDEO WHILE ON A FACETIME CALL ON IOS 14 AND OLDER

1. Establish or accept a FaceTime call.
2. Access more choices by swiping up from the toolbar's base.
3. When you're done recording, tap the Camera Off toggle to stop recording.

The other party on the call will still be able to hear your voice, but your video will cease.

HOW TO USE SIRI TO PLACE A FACETIME CALL

1. On iPhones that have a Home button, press and hold it. On iPhones with Face ID, press and hold the Side button. Or, just say "Hey Siri" to activate Siri.
2. "Facetime [name]" is expressed. You could also just say "FaceTime" and wait for Siri to give you the name of your contact to follow.

Just wait for Siri to establish the connection now.

HOW TO USE FACETIME WITH APPLE TV
1. From the bottom of your screen, swipe up (for iPhones with Home buttons) or from the right corner of your Home screen (for iPhones with Face ID), depending on which one you're using.
2. Navigate to the Screen Mirroring option.
3. Select the device whose screen you want to mirror from your iPhone.

Then, all you have to do is follow the on-screen instructions to make a FaceTime call on your iPhone.

CHAPTER ELEVEN

HOW TO ORGANIZE PHOTOS ON IPHONE

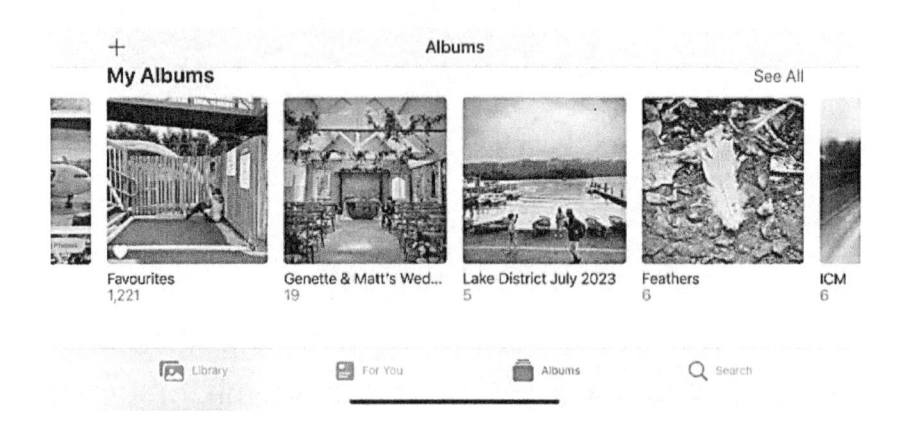

An absolute game-changer is the ability to organize your iPhone images into albums. You can arrange your iPhone images in albums and do things like:

- Assign categories to your media files according to your tastes.
- Add depth and structure to your collection
- Quickly locate a particular wedding photo—not minutes—from your cousin's big day.

You can make this a reality with structured albums, which make creating albums a breeze.

Your iPhone will automatically generate albums depending on the kind of media, but you can also build custom albums to better organize your images. That's right! Live images, Selfies, and Portrait are just a few of the albums that your iPhone's Photos app will automatically organize your images into. When you utilize smart albums in conjunction with personalized albums, sharing and retrieving your memories will be a snap.

Discovering Your Way Around The Photos App

In the Photos app on an iPhone, you may find four main sections: Library, For You, Albums, and Search. The Library tab is a great place to organize all of your pictures and events by year, month, and day. By clicking the Filters button and choosing an option, you may further simplify the process of finding certain photographs on the Library page.

A curated collection of your most treasured experiences may be found under the "For You" page. Memories are collections of images and movies from certain events or times that it found by searching across your media library, even including duplicates. You may watch highlight reels of your most treasured memories here. All of your picture and video albums, including shared albums and your creations, may be found under the Albums tab.

Another great feature is iCloud Photos, which allows you to sync your photo albums across all of your Apple devices. All of your devices will automatically reflect any changes you make to your albums, so your memories are always accessible and up-to-date.

Custom picture albums are a great way to organize and simplify your iPhone photographs by grouping them by topic, occasion, or place. Using this strategy, finding and sharing certain photographs becomes much easier.

First, we'll examine how to put images into custom albums. Then, we'll rename and alter the albums.

ADDING PHOTOS TO CUSTOM ALBUMS

Adding images to your albums is as easy as following these steps:

1. To begin, use the Photos app and touch on the photos you want to use.
2. A menu of choices will be shown when you tap the three-dot symbol (upper right).

3. Click the "Add to Album" button.

4. Click "New Album" to start a new album, or choose an existing album to transfer the images to. Select "Save" once you've entered the name of the album.

5. To complete adding photographs to your albums, repeat the procedure.

Adding several photographs at once is as easy as:

1. Launch the Photos app and locate the Select icon in the upper right corner.
2. After that, choose the images you want to include in an album by tapping on them. Each chosen picture will get a blue checkmark in its corner.

3. To access the menu, tap the three dots in the lower right corner. Click the "Add to Album" button.
4. Just like previously, choose an existing album or make a new one to which you'd want to add the images.

You may quickly access the album to which you have recently contributed images by tapping "Albums" in the upper left corner of the photo roll. You can see all of your current albums in one place. From that location, you may effortlessly access your album. Under the "My Albums" tab up top, you should be able to find it. To open a certain album, just swipe your finger across the screen. Press the "See All" button if you can't see it. Press the name of the album. To access the photographs included therein, just click on them.

Editing And Renaming Personal Albums

Making changes to your albums is easy. This is how you rename an album:

1. Navigate to the Albums page.
2. In the "My Albums" area, tap "See All."

3. Look for the "Edit" button in the upper right corner.

183

4. Select the album whose name you want to edit.

5. Use the keyboard to enter a new name.

6. To commit the modifications, tap "Done."

In this way, you may maintain an orderly and current picture book even as your photo collection expands.

It is very simple to edit personalized albums. If you want to delete images from an album but keep them in your library, you may do it like this:

1. Turn on the album.
2. By tapping "Select," you may choose which photographs to delete.

3. Press the bin icon.
4. Go to the "Remove from Album" menu.

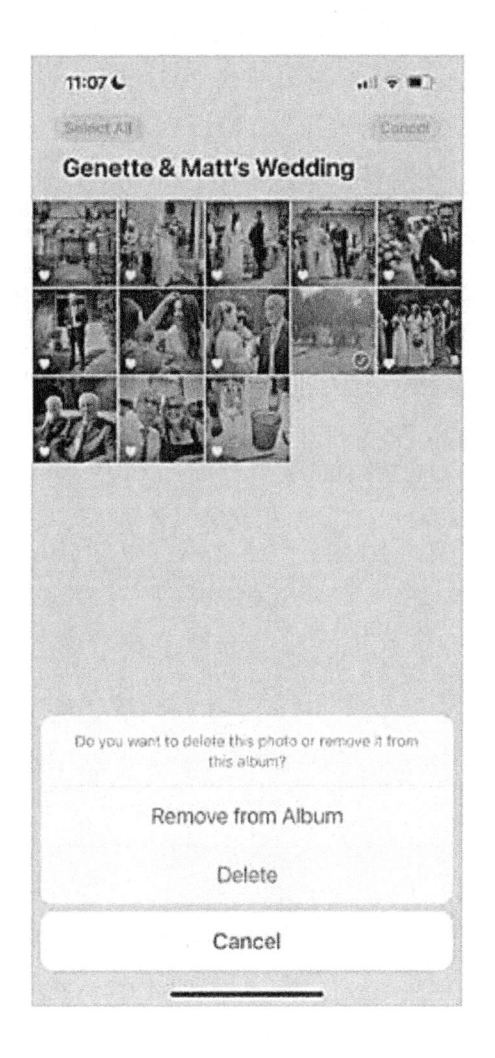

Please follow these instructions to add more photographs to an album:

    1. Hover over the ellipsis symbol (three dots).

2. Click on "Add Photos" to continue.

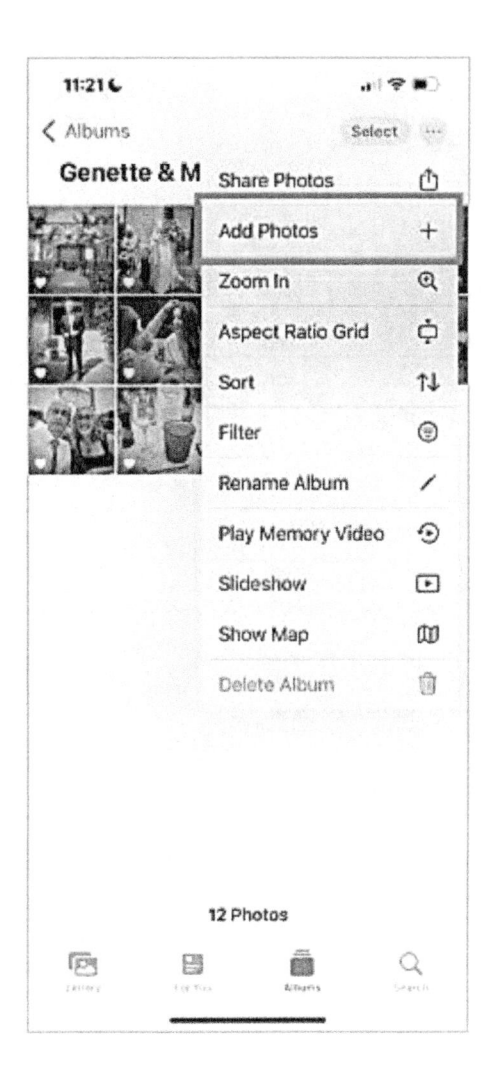

3. Insert photographs by browsing your photo library.
4. To add images to the album once you've chosen them, press "Add" in the top right corner.

REMOVING DUPLICATE OR UNWANTED PHOTOS

Decluttering your picture collection and making room for more is as simple as removing duplicates and unneeded photographs. Save a copy of your images to a different location, either locally or on the cloud, before you erase them. Doing so will aid you in preventing the unintentional deletion of any treasured memories.

Delete several images at once by following these steps:

1. Launch Media Library.
2. To see the full-sized images, switch to thumbnail view.
3. Click the "Select" button in the upper right.

4. To remove certain images, select them all.

5. Select the "Delete" (trash) icon.

6. Lastly, confirm the deletion by hitting the Delete Photos button.

The Recently Deleted album will then include all of the erased photographs.

MANAGING THE RECENTLY DELETED ALBUM

You may temporarily save your deleted photos in the Recently Deleted album, but they will be completely removed after 30 days. You may use this program to recover photos that you accidentally erased or those you want to permanently eliminate to make more space on your iPhone.

Simply choose an image to recover from the album labeled "Recently Deleted" and then click the "Recover" button. To permanently delete images from the Recently Deleted album, press Select. You may delete them all by clicking the Delete All button. The photos in the Recently Deleted album will be erased after 30 days, so please be aware of that.

Photo Tagging And Finding

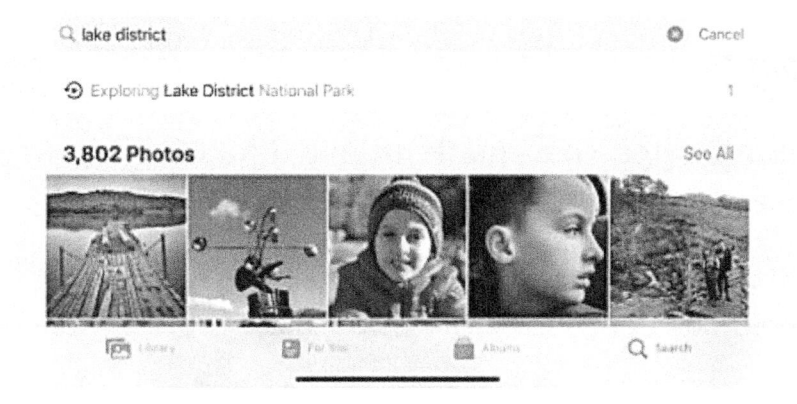

A great approach to organizing and discovering certain photographs in your collection is to tag them with keywords. If you tag individuals in your images with names, you can quickly see all the ones that include that person. Including geotags with your images is a great way to keep track of where you shot each shot.

The following are the procedures to take to locate certain photographs on the photographs app:

1. Please choose the Search tab.
2. To begin searching, enter the name or term you want to use.
3. You won't have to go through your whole collection to get the precise picture you need thanks to the search tool.

USING ICLOUD FOR PHOTO SYNC AND SHARING

With iCloud, syncing and sharing your Apple pictures across all of your devices is a breeze. All of your Apple devices will have access to your photo albums after you enable iCloud Photos. This way, your memories are never far away.

Here are the procedures to take to see whether other Apple devices may access your iCloud Photos albums:

1. Select Photos from the iCloud menu in the Settings app on your iOS device.
2. Navigate to Apple ID > iCloud in System Preferences on a Mac.
3. You need to turn on Photos.
4. See all of your connected albums in the Photos app's My Albums section.

With iCloud, you can not only sync your media across all of your devices but also send individual media files or whole albums to certain recipients. Another option is to create a shared album and invite others to contribute images, videos, and comments. Use this function to tell your loved ones about special occasions or vacations you've been on.

CHAPTER TWELVE

TIPS AND TRICKS

1. Put Many Applications Into A Folder With A Single Drag.

By touching and holding one icon, dragging it, and then tapping on additional icons while holding it, you may effortlessly move many programs into a single folder. After you've selected all the extra applications you want to transfer, just drop the collection into an existing folder.

2. Avoid Charging Over 80%

If you want your battery to last as long as possible in good condition, charging it to 80% and stopping there is one strategy. You can now accomplish this using an iOS setting. To enable it, go to Settings > Battery > Battery Health and Charging. Then, choose Charging Optimisation on the subsequent page. From the available choices, choose the 80% limit.

3. A Simple Push Of A Button May Create The Sound Of Rain.

In iOS, you may create ambient noises by pressing the side button three times in quick succession. To begin, go to Settings > Accessibility > Audio/Vision and then pick Background Sounds to choose the sound you want to use. Press "Sound" now, and then choose an effect from the drop-down menu.

Return to the list of Accessibility options on your iPhone and touch "Accessibility Shortcut" to allow the ability to launch that sound using the side key. Pick "Background Sounds" from the drop-down menu; then, triple-clicking the side key will trigger the playing of your selected sound.

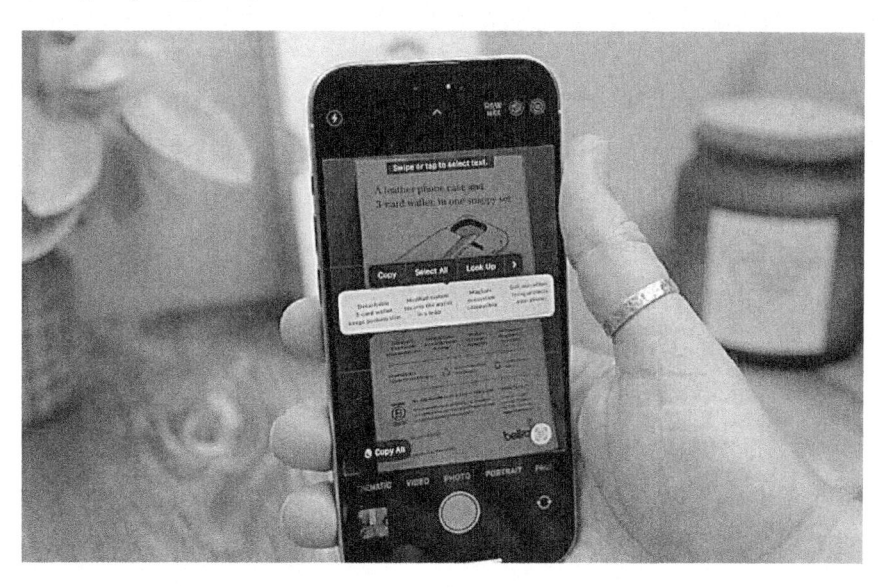

4. **Take A Picture Of Text And Have It Translated Using The Camera App For IOS.**

The camera has an automated detection function that can tell whether you're aiming it at text. Once your phone detects text in the camera view, a little indicator like three lines within an outlined square will display. A selection of options, including copy, paste, search, translate, and share, will appear when you tap that icon once it has grabbed the text. Even better, you can use the drag-and-drop feature to select text and then apply the same actions to it.

5. The Most Straightforward Method For Cropping Images

On the iPhone, cropping is a breeze, saving you the trouble of going through all the editing choices. To zoom in until the corners of the screen meet, just open the desired picture in Photos, pinch to zoom, and then release the screen. Hit the "Crop" button in the upper right corner after you've adjusted the size to your liking. Alternatively, you may press and hold the button to choose a predetermined ratio and then hit "Crop" to apply it. Press "done" when you're satisfied.

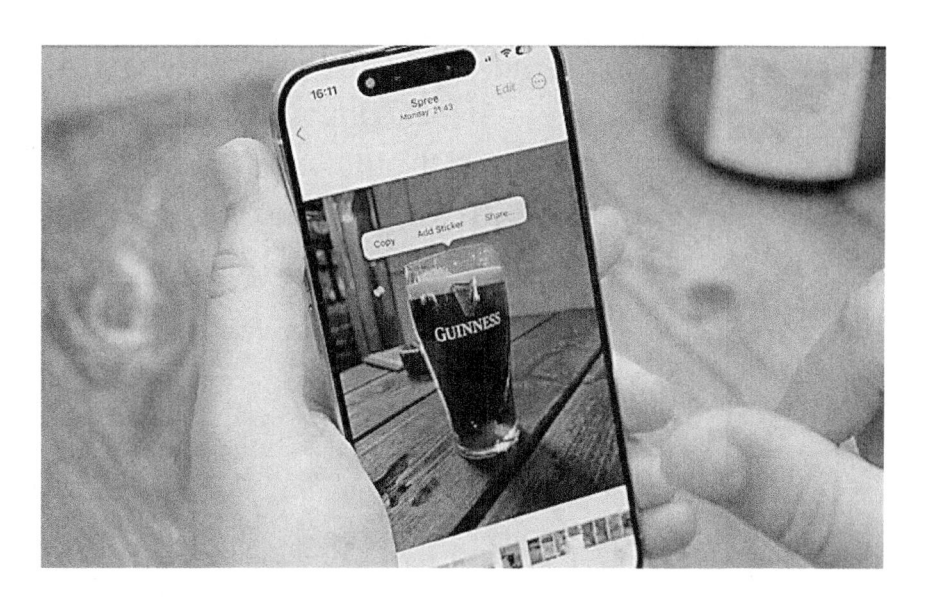

6. Make A Custom Sticker Using Any Image

The option to make one's iMessage stickers is new to iOS 17. One easier way to produce them is to use the Photos app instead of the Messages app.

To do this, just pull up a picture of a topic in the foreground in your iPhone's Photos app. Once you've removed the subject from its backdrop, press and hold it until you see the glowing lines. Select an effect, then press "add sticker" in the pop-up menu.

7. Get Apple Maps Offline

You may now download certain places to use for offline navigation using the latest version of Apple Maps. Launch Maps, then choose "offline maps" by tapping your profile picture in the upper right area of the preview window. Select "download new map," enter a search term, pinch to zoom, adjust the region size, and finally, press "Download."

8. Research Laundry Care Symbols

Thanks to iOS 17, Visual Look Up is now smarter and can identify a wider variety of objects than before, including plants, animals, and historical sites. Take a picture of a laundry care label, for instance. On the bottom toolbar, you'll see the Visual Look Up 'i' icon with stars. Tap on it. From the pop-up menu, pick Visual Look Up. This will show you the meaning of the symbols on that particular label.

9. Make Use Of The Apple Logo As A Hidden Dial

By touching the back of the phone, close to the Apple logo, you may access many functions, including taking screenshots, if the appropriate settings are enabled. Press Touch, then Back Tap, under the Settings menu, under Accessibility. Now choose an action to do with the double tap; I went with a Screenshot, but you may pick whatever you desire. To make it a triple tap, you may also add one.

10.   A Set Of Labeled Timers

Do you need a plethora of timers, each with its label? Sure thing. Press "Start" after opening the clock, selecting "timers," entering a new time, editing the label, and finalizing your work. Press the plus sign in the upper right, and then repeat the process for the next timed item. Use this method to add an unlimited number.

Just say "Set an 8-minute 'eggs' timer" followed by "Set a 29-minute fries timer" and have Siri take care of it automatically. Or whenever you'd want. An assortment of timers, each with a unique label, may be neatly stacked.

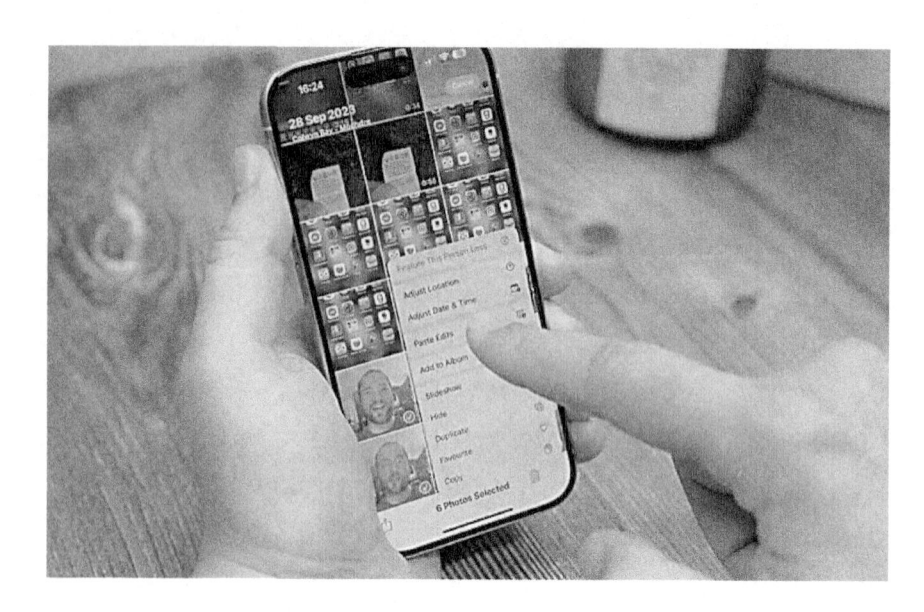

11. Edit Photos By Copying And Pasting.

There is a simple technique to apply the same adjustments to many photos at once, rather than having to go through each one individually. Start by modifying an existing picture. After you've added all of your desired filters and effects, save the file.

From the menu that appears, choose "Copy Edits" after tapping the three dots in the upper right corner. Return to your library and choose "Select" from the menu at the top. Press the three dots in the bottom corner and choose "Paste Edits." All the photographs you've chosen will be transformed into the style you want.

12. Only Available In 15 Pro And 15 Pro Max, Shoot In LOG.

Apple added the option to shoot in Log on the iPhone 15 Pro, providing color graders with extra color data to work with. Go to "Settings" > "Camera" > "Formats," then choose "ProRes Encoding" after toggling the "ProRes" option at the bottom. Choose 'Log' from the subsequent screen.

Go ahead and launch the camera. Select the video mode and then locate the 'Log' option on the top toolbar. When you're ready to start recording, press the record button. Keep in mind that some resolutions and frame rates may need an external SSD to be attached.

After filming, the finished product may seem colorless and flat; nevertheless, there is a great deal of leeway when editing the video by adjusting the hues, saturation, lightness, and darkness.

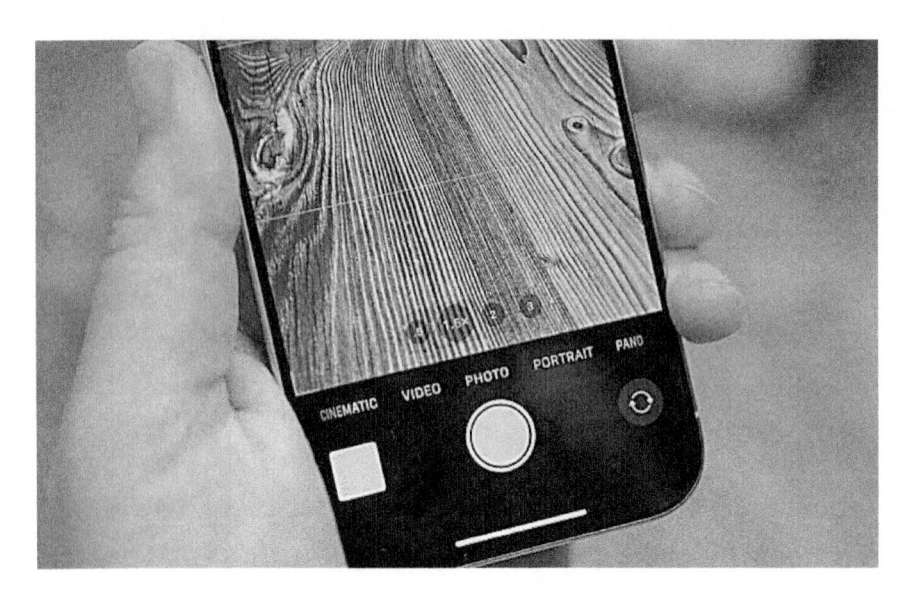

13. Alter The Lens Length Of Your Main Camera.

The default setting for the main camera on the iPhone 15 Pro is a wide 24mm focal length equivalent, but you have the option to change it. Navigate to Settings > Camera and locate 'Main Camera' to choose a smaller field of vision as your default. In place of the broader 24mm lens, choose the default setting; from now on, whenever you launch the camera app, that setting will be the primary choice.

14. Keyboard Trackpad

The iPhone's built-in touchpad is an old favorite of mine. To transform the whole area into a touchpad and move the pointer precisely where you want it to, hit and hold the space bar while typing. The keyboard will then fade out, and you can use your thumb to slide it around.

Printed in Great Britain
by Amazon